Patterns in Ibsen's Middle Plays

Also by **Richard Hornby:**

Script into Performance: A Structuralist View of Play Production

Patterns in Ibsen's Middle Plays

Richard Hornby

Lewisburg
Bucknell University Press
London and Toronto: Associated University Presses

© 1981 by Associated University Presses, Inc.

Associated University Presses, Inc.
4 Cornwall Drive
East Brunswick, N. J. 08816

Associated University Presses Ltd.
69 Fleet Street
London EC4Y 1EU, England

Associated University Presses
Toronto, Ontario, Canada M5E 1A7

Library of Congress Cataloging in Publication Data

Hornby, Richard, 1938-
   Patterns in Ibsen's middle plays.

   Bibliography: p.
   Includes index.
   1. Ibsen, Henrik, 1828-1906—Criticism and interpretation.   I. Title.
PT8895.H67   839.8'226   80-67969
ISBN 0-8387-5014-1

Printed in the United States of America

Contents

Acknowledgments
1. A Structuralist Approach to Ibsen — 13
2. Ibsen's Allegorical Realism — 33
3. *Brand* and *Peer Gynt:* Ibsen's *Either/Or* — 53
4. The Ethical Leap: *A Doll House* — 89
5. The Tragedy of the Aesthetic Life: *Ghosts* — 120
6. The Validity of the Ironic Life: *An Enemy of the People* — 147
7. Reflections on Art and Politics — 180
   Notes — 185
   Bibliography — 189
   Index — 194

To all the Students and Professors in the
Theatre Department of Tulane University, 1963–1966

Acknowledgments

We are now blessed with a number of good English translations of Ibsen's playscripts. The Oxford *Ibsen,* edited by James Walter McFarlane and with most of the translations by him as well, is highly regarded for thoroughness—even Ibsen's early drafts are included—and literal accuracy, but not so much for poetic sensitivity or speakable dialogue. Therefore, since one of the aims of this book is to affect the practical theater, I have instead made use of the admirable translations of Michael Meyer and Rolf Fjelde. Their translations are lucid and vigorous, and have been successfully tested many times onstage. Although slightly freer than the Oxford versions, they stay close to the original, in contrast to the unfortunate stage adaptations (often put together from several sources by people who do not know Norwegian) that are becoming common.

Specifically, the quotations from *Brand* are from Henrik Ibsen, *Brand,* translated by Michael Meyer (Garden City, N.Y.: Doubleday, 1960); those from *Peer Gynt* from Henrik Ibsen, *Peer Gynt,* translated by Rolf Fjelde (New York: New American Library, 1965); and those from *A Doll House, Ghosts,* and *An Enemy of the People* from Henrik Ibsen, *Ibsen: The Complete Major Prose Plays,* translated and introduced by Rolf Fjelde (New York: Farrar, Straus & Giroux, 1978). Page references hereinafter given in the text are to these editions. Both Mr. Meyer and Professor Fjelde have generously given their permissions to allow me to quote from their translations. Readers are warned that these are fully protected under copyright.

In addition, I am especially indebted to Professor Fjelde for helping me with the original Norwegian. While this book is definitely not a linguistic study, and while the major elements in the playscripts are eminently translatable (Captain Alving's pipe is a pipe, regardless of translator), there were points where I could not avoid discussing some nuance of expression or pattern of imagery that had to be checked with the original.

An example of such nuance is the title *A Doll House*, which may give pause to some readers. Professor Fjelde in his introduction to the play gives two reasons for preferring this translation of *Et Dukkehjem* to the more common *A Doll's House:* first of all, it is not possessive in the original, but more important, "it is the entire house (*hjem*, home) which is on trial, the total complex of relationships. . . . No character is superfluous in the design, nor negligible in performance" (p. 121). I could not agree more; in fact, it is that very "complex of relationships" that I try to explicate.

Finally, I wish the thank the Publications Committee of the University of Calgary for providing a subvention grant to assist in the publication of this book.

1/A Structuralist Approach to Ibsen

TRADITIONAL dramatic criticism, based in Aristotle, has tended to be atomistic. Aristotle spoke of the "parts" of a play, such as plot, characters, and theme; even where subsequent critics have given these parts different names, or spoken of entirely different parts, they have still tended to treat plays as piecemeal collections of elements, each of which exists in isolation. A social theme is seen as separate from a personal problem; characterization is discussed as if it had nothing to do with setting or plot; an aesthetic motif is taken to preclude a political message; a style is categorized as "realistic" or "Romantic," but not both. The play, dissected and examined, becomes a dead artifact. Themes, characterizations, plots, motifs, styles, ideas, myths, images are just "there," as tangible as potatoes, which the critic packages for easy delivery to readers and audiences, who receive the play but contribute nothing to it.

Because of this traditional, atomistic approach, the plays of Ibsen's middle period have been a special problem for critics. *A Doll House, Ghosts, An Enemy of the People*—are these social pamphlets or works of art? Are politics and art antithetical, as some writers have insisted? Is it necessary to be a Marxist-Leninist, seeing "drama as a weapon," in order to accept Ibsen as an important playwright? Or, conversely, is it necessary to ignore the sociopolitical elements in Ibsen as if they were an embarrassment, detracting from his plays as "art"? Is Ibsen a bourgeois playwright glorifying the individual, or is he a left-wing radical calling for drastic social change? Can a playwright be both an artist *and* a pamphleteer?

There is a way out of this maze of dichotomies. In recent years, literary criticism has been changing drastically. Structuralism, a contemporary mode of thought with wide-ranging applications, has affected its techniques. The change is not simply one of viewpoint, like so many changes in the past, as the fads of historical, rhetorical, imagistic, psychoanalytic, Marxist, anthropological, and mythic criticisms waxed and waned. Structuralism transcends such particularities; it represents a change in the very style of criticism.

This new style is epitomized in (though hardly limited to) the theories of the critic Roman Jakobson. Jakobson has been influential in the three most noted schools of Structuralism: Born in Moscow in 1894, he was one of the early Russian Formalists; moving to Prague in 1920, he brought the ideas of the Formalists to the Prague Linguistic Circle of Structuralists; leaving Czechoslovakia in the year of Hitler's takeover, he moved to New York City, where he met, and influenced, the French Structuralist Claude Lévi-Strauss. (The two eventually collaborated on a famous Structuralist essay on Baudelaire's poem "Les Chats.") Thus the seminal nature of Jakobson's thought can hardly be overestimated.

The culminating idea of Jakobson's has been his formulation of the act of communication,[1] showing it to involve six related factors, which he arranges triadically:

CONTEXT

ADDRESSER MESSAGE ADDRESSEE

CONTACT

CODE

the important thing to recognize is that the *message,* sent from the addresser to the addressee, is never the total *meaning*. Instead, meaning is embodied in the entire system; meaning in fact changes when any of the six factors is changed.

In the case of drama, the *addresser* would be the playwright; the message, the play itself; the *addressee,* the audience member or reader. Most people would accept the idea that changing playwright or play alters meaning (although in the case of the latter, some directors do seem to feel, oddly, that they can make drastic changes in the play and still have it mean the same). A more interesting point is that, for Jakobson, each individual addressee has, in a sense, his own play. Furthermore, the meaning of that play changes with every reading, or viewing, as *context, contact,* and *code* change.

The *context* includes the whole sociohistorical complex within which the play takes place. It strongly affects the addressee's experience of the play, so that, for example, it is possible for Shakespeare to be "our contemporary," *not* because Shakespeare wrote with a prescient eye on the twentieth century, but because differing circumstances develop or obscure differing relationships within the play, thus creating new patterns of significance. Shylock, for example, becomes a very different figure when viewed in the context of twentieth-century Nazism from what he was in Shakespeare's time.

The *contact* is the means of communication, and, again, the experience of a play is different when read from what it is when seen on stage, and different again when seen on film. In fact, since performances vary from night to night in the theater, even in a meticulous production, each performance of a play will carry a slightly different meaning.

The *code,* finally, is the system of thought by which we interpret what we see or read. Code is the central concern of *criticism;* indeed, it is its very reason for being. Each critical approach decodes the play for us in a different way. Thus, the psychoanalytic critic shows us a different

Hamlet from that of the historical critic, who shows us a different *Hamlet* from that of the anthropological critic. A traditional critic, of course, may not believe that he is employing a code, but think instead that he is merely pointing out tangible, fixed truths. But instead of taking this simple-minded view, where the meaning of a play is simply "there," to be handed over to the reader or audience member by the obliging critic, we need to see criticism as an active, creative act, a construction of a model of a play in a kind of collaboration with the playwright. New critics find new codes, which create new models. This is why criticism continues indefinitely; there is literally no end to writing new things about *Hamlet,* or any other great play.

The play itself, then, should not be viewed as a collection of fixed entities, whether those entities are characters, or themes, or ideas, or anything else. Rather, the elements in a play should be seen as essentially interrelated, in an immensely complex web. Differing approaches, or "codes," expose differing structures in these relationships, so that the play, although finite, can provide a theoretically infinite number of interpretations, or "decodings." The reader or audience member in a sense *completes* a brand-new structure with every reading or viewing, as a function of the code under which he operates; he is not a mere passive recipient but rather an active collaborator. The critic, instead of simply telling the reader or audience member "what the play means," discovers or creates codes to the play that will enlarge the reader's or audience member's thought system and thus broaden and intensify his experience of the art work. Rather than simply being told about the work, the reader or audience member is given the means to *do* something with it.

A work of traditional dramatic criticism usually presented the reader/audience member with a *single* interpretation. That is, employing a single "code" or approach, the critic decoded the text in a way that was supposed to be fixed and final. Unfortunately, however, such fixed interpretations came to change and be supplanted with the passing of time. Thus, with Ibsen, English-speaking critics like Shaw and Archer first employed a sociopolitical code. Ibsen's plays were looked upon as pamphlets or sermons on social issues like women's rights, free speech, syphilis, or water pollution. Given the historical context of Victorian social reform movements, this made Ibsen into a sensational playwright. His reputation in the English-speaking world in the late nineteenth century was so powerful that if one were asked to name the most significant and influential "English" playwright of the period, one would have to say "Ibsen." His plays are still commonly included in English literature courses in universities, as if he were one of our own. But in the 1920s, his reputation went into a decline; social protest literature had become passé. The social problems that had obsessed the Victorians were supposedly all solved—did not women have the vote?—and the "problem play" was now of only historical interest. In Structuralist terms, one could say that the code had not changed (the plays were still being seen in terms of social protest), but the historical *context* had changed, and Ibsen became devalued.

Then, after the Second World War, there began a revaluation of Ibsen's drama, starting with M. C. Bradbrook's *Ibsen the Norwegian* (1946), and continuing through such critical works as Brian Downs's *Ibsen: The Intellectual Background* (1946), John Northam's *Ibsen's Dramatic Method* (1953), and G. Wilson Knight's *Henrik Ibsen* (1962). These critics generally viewed Ibsen not as a social reformer at all, but rather as a poet, both in the linguistic sense (he wrote a fair amount of nondramatic poetry, a third of his plays are in verse, and his prose plays, according to some, display a poetic sensitivity to language), and in the figurative sense of being concerned with fundamental issues of life, death, guilt, love, and personal freedom. Slow at first, the revaluation has snowballed to the point where hardly a year goes by now without the publication of another book, in English, that treats Ibsen as a sensitive and profound artist. In Structuralist terms, not only has the *context* changed, but the *code* for interpreting the plays has changed, from a sociopolitical code to an aesthetic one.

The trouble is that the new code/context has completely supplanted the old. Ibsen critics now generally reject the sociopolitical approach entirely, in favor of the new poetic approach. This has made it difficult to deal with the plays of Ibsen's middle period, where the political content seems unavoidable. The result is that the relative popularity of Ibsen's various plays has completely turned around since Archer's and Shaw's day. Consider, for example, three of the best Ibsen books of the 1970s: Orley I. Holtan's *Mythic Patterns in Ibsen's Late Plays* (1970), Charles R. Lyons's *Henrik Ibsen: The Divided Consciousness* (1972), and John Northam's *Ibsen: A Critical Study* (1973). Each in its own way is a sensitive and often ingenious study, yet each also avoids the social plays of the middle period as if they were an embarrassment, detracting from the critic's vision of the "true," poetical Ibsen. The Holtan book, as one could infer from the title, starts with *The Wild Duck* and moves forward; although Holtan believes that myth exists in the plays of the middle period, it does so for him only in an enfeebled manner, "displaced behind a façade of direct concern with social problems."[2] With plays like *A Doll House, Ghosts,* and *An Enemy of the People,* the remnants of the Shaw/Archer approach are still strong enough to "displace" Holtan's interest, although a mythical approach to these plays might prove very fruitful. The Lyons book jumps right over the middle period, skipping from *Em-*

peror and Galilean to *The Wild Duck*.³ The Northam book deals with only one middle play, *Ghosts*,⁴ no doubt partly because it is the least easily categorizable as a "problem play." In an earlier book, Northam denounced *An Enemy of the People*, more clearly a problem play, as "the least imaginative of all Ibsen's prose dramas."⁵ It is ironic that the very plays that gave Ibsen his reputation in the English-speaking world now rate the lowest among critics, who have come to prefer the Romantic early plays, and the "poetic" late ones; the Ibsen of Shaw and Archer has been turned on his head.

This book decidedly does not attempt to present yet another exclusivist interpretation of Ibsen, which would lead, as these other critical studies have tended to do, to a *narrowing* of our vision of his plays. The Structuralist critic, instead of allowing one critical approach to displace another, takes an essentially pluralist position toward a literary work. The French Structuralist Roland Barthes, for example, in his book *S/Z*, examines a realistic story by Balzac in terms of five codes⁶—a code of actions, a code of puzzles, a cultural code, a connotative code, a symbolic code. Each code is a system that generates meaning when placed against the text—that is, when the text is decoded. Barthes's five codes generate no less than ninety-three meanings of Balzac's story! Obviously, more meanings, and even more codes, are possible. Reading the short story with Barthes's guidance thus becomes an *open* experience; in fact, with each reading we are creating a brand new story, as we find new applications for Barthes's codes that he himself may not have noticed. Nor is there any reason why we cannot simultaneously bring in other codes as well; the vision of the story that Barthes's engenders will be enhanced, rather than displaced, by additional interpretations.

Pluralism of interpretation does not mean, however,

that all possible interpretations of a literary work are correct. Of course, any interpretation must be tested against the work itself; on the evidence, some interpretations may be found to have extensive application throughout the work, some to have only narrow validity, and some to be dead wrong. But any great work of art will allow for a limitless number of sound, potent interpretations. Some of these may even contradict each other; thus, Samuel Beckett's *Waiting for Godot* has been interpreted both as a gloomy piece of existentialism denying all meaning to life, and as an optimistic play about man's capacity for hope. Such a contradiction should not be taken as prima facie evidence that one or the other of the interpretations is wrong; assuming that both can be supported by evidence from the play's text, contradictory interpretations should instead stimulate our appreciation of the play's energy and mystery.

The Structuralist critic, then, sees the literary text as an interrelated process open to interpretation from a limitless number of approaches, in a limitless number of contexts; he elaborates some of these approaches or "codes," and explicates many meanings from his own personal context, but he makes it clear that no meaning is "the truth." He points the way; he does not pin down. The reader uses the work of literary criticism as a kind of guidebook for his own active confrontation with the literary text, recognizing that the critical work, like all guidebooks, is merely introductory and incomplete.

This book will examine Ibsen's middle plays in terms of three principal codes: a philosophical code, a stylistic code, and a theatrical code. Like Barthes in *S/Z*, I shall be focusing on works that are widely considered to be blunt, straightforward, and realistic. My thesis is that this view, while not wrong, is limited; it takes a single, stylistic code in a single, historical context and yields a single, clear, accurate interpretation that is circumscribed and shallow. The very accuracy of the sociopolitical interpretation has, ironically, desensitized people to Ibsen's middle plays. The purpose of my interpretation, on the other hand, is not to pin down Ibsen's meanings, but rather to sensitize readers to the multiplicity of meanings that are possible. In substituting three new codes for the traditional one, I am not rejecting previous criticism, but instead enlarging it.

An example of how Ibsen could simultaneously write a social protest play and a personal play of individual heroism can be seen in *A Doll House*. Nora Helmer is in one sense a victim of a male-chauvinist society, unable even to take a bank loan without a man's counter-signature, reduced to a doll-like existence by her loving and well-meaning (and therefore all the more repressive) father and husband. But on the other hand, it is her father and husband that she is reacting to, and not "men" in the abstract, and she took the bank loan, in a stroke of irony, in order to save her darling husband's life. One can well imagine a television situation comedy in which a character like Maude Findley or Gloria Stivak takes out a loan to go to college or to start a business—in other words to advance *herself* as an independent person—only to be squelched by a series of stereotyped bank managers and businessmen. But Nora does not inhabit a world of stereotypes; her opponents are all complex and generally well-meaning individuals. In fact, her major opponent is herself, since she has always acquiesced and even delighted in her doll existence. In Marx's terms, her consciousness has been formed by her material condition, rather than being, as in simplistic social drama, detached from her condition and in simple opposition to it. The greatness of *A Doll House* lies in its openness to a multiplicity of interpretations, unlike simple works like television comedies or Soviet tractor plays that operate only on a few obvious levels. It is wrong to see *A Doll House* in purely personal terms—in a society in which women could borrow money on their own, for example, Nora would never have had to forge her father's signature, and would never have got into trouble—but it is also wrong to see the play as a purely abstract question of issues. Nora's leaving her husband can be seen as a blow for women's rights, with Nora standing for "the liberated woman" and Helmer for "the repressive male-chauvinist"; and it can simultaneously be seen as a terrible personal crisis, with Nora tearing herself from a husband whom she once loved and from children whom she still does love. Ultimately, issues and people are so intertwined in the play as to be inseparable. Even in a play as outrightly polemical as *An Enemy of the People,* the social struggle has its counterpart, as I shall attempt to show, in the personal struggles among highly individualized characters, as well as in a private conflict within the central character.

But even this kind of interpretation is inadequate. In demonstrating that Nora's struggle can be interpreted in both personal and sociopolitical terms, I have treated the character in isolation, which is, again, a technique of traditional rather than Structuralist criticism. Structuralism treats the elements of a literary work as interconnected. Nora's characterization—or, indeed, any element of the play—must be seen in terms of some underlying structure that in some way informs the play as a whole. The play is then conceived of not as a piecemeal collection of characters or problems or ideas, but rather as an interrelated process that moves us in totality. Unless we treat a play in this holistic fashion, we end up, as traditional criticism so often does, as if we were trying to deduce the essential nature of Niagara Falls from a bucket of water taken from the Niagara River. A play exhibits form in *motion;* indeed, it becomes a living thing, even in reading, when we respond to it. We do not go to see *A Doll House* in order to "examine" Nora, as if we were her psychoanalyst, nor to learn new ideas about women's rights or some other issue. Instead, we go for an *experience,* as living, active, responsive human beings. The experience incorporates elements like character and theme, but its essential nature is very different from any of its constituent parts considered individually, because it is a *structure* that we are responding to. Music provides a clearer example of this. A melody that is played an octave higher than it is written, so that all the notes are literally different, is still recognizable as the same melody because the structure is the same; a melody whose structure is rearranged, even if the very same notes are used, sounds different. The problem with dramatic criticism is that, where in music B-flat by itself means nothing, in drama individual elements can have meaning, and can thus be isolated and discussed. Nevertheless, a dramatic critic who does so isolate and discuss is as false to the essence of drama as a music critic would be to the essence of music if he were to catalogue all the notes of Beethoven's Fifth Symphony and proceed to discuss them individually. In drama as in music, as indeed in all the arts, one must consider individual parts in terms of their relationships to one another, in overall structures.

Thus, in interpreting Ibsen's middle plays, I shall be explicating multiple, overlapping patterns, often through the use of charts. While of course I shall not be able to avoid talking, from time to time, about elements of the plays in isolation (as in the discussion of Nora, above), the reader should try not to consider such discussions out of the context of the larger structures. This is an important rule for all dramatic criticism, but especially for that dealing with Ibsen, whose control of detail is extraordinary, and whose structures, although subtle, can leap out with astonishing force when properly decoded.

The primary code I shall be employing to explicate Ibsen's structures is based on the terminology of the Danish philosopher and near contemporary of Ibsen, Søren Kierkegaard. I must stress, however, that this is not the same thing as saying that Ibsen is a Kierkegaardian playwright, or that his plays are full of Kierkegaardian philosophy. To do so would be to confuse code with message. As a matter of fact, Ibsen was not particularly philosophical, and his plays, again, impress audiences not so much by the philosophies or "issues" that critics have attached to them as by the virtual life of the characters that they depict. But the vividness of that life in turn arises from a certain view of human nature, widely held in the nineteenth century, which Kierkegaard articulated in a special way, and which Ibsen, consciously or unconsciously, shared.

The connection between Kierkegaard and Ibsen has never been adequately explored, partly because other approaches to Ibsen, even when valid, have tended to obscure alternatives, but also because Ibsen himself specifically disclaimed any Kierkegaardian influence. Ibsen's denials in this matter are certainly vehement, and for some critics they have settled the point completely. For example, in a passage from one of his letters that has often been quoted, he remarked that certain people had detected a similarity between the character of Brand in Ibsen's play and the personality of Kierkegaard himself. Ibsen wrote:

> It is a great mistake to suppose that I have depicted the life and career of Kierkegaard (I have read very little of Kierkegaard and understood even less). That Brand is a clergyman is really immaterial.[7]

But we should not set too great store on such disclaimers. For one thing, even if Ibsen had read very little of Kierkegaard, playwrights often receive ideas at second hand—as Eugene O'Neill did with Freud, for example—and certainly Kierkegaard's ideas had been "in the air" among Scandinavian intellectuals throughout Ibsen's formative years. Alternatively, if Ibsen was *not* being truthful here, and had actually read Kierkegaard extensively, it would have been characteristic of him to deny it. Eva Le Gallienne has noted Ibsen's "pettiness in refusing to acknowledge the slightest external influence on his work."[8] We must remember that it was the mode in Ibsen's time to consider poets, playwrights, and other literary artists as original thinkers; our modern concept of the artist as a detached observer rather than a social and moral commentator is a product of the realistic movement that was then in its infancy. Ibsen probably regarded the suggestion of a Kierkegaardian influence, which to us seems perfectly natural and even admirable in a creative writer, as a charge of plagiarism.

But ultimately the question of the historical link between Kierkegaard and Ibsen is moot. Plays are not embellished philosophies, but rather organic complexes in which characters, actions, and ideas are interrelated in a holistic vision of life. Philosophies are useful in helping to understand plays, and not the other way around—at least, if one genuinely wants to be a dramatic critic, rather than a historian of ideas. These are points that many traditional critics overlook; they claim exclusivity for some particular philosopher for the interpretation of some particular play, not realizing that in so doing they are reducing the playwright to being the philosopher's mouthpiece. In a recent book, *The Ibsen Cycle,* Brian Johnston makes an excellent case for viewing the twelve plays from *Pillars of Society* to *When We Dead Awaken* as a reflection of Hegel's cyclic and evolutionary view of history. Unfortunately, Johnston's book is marred by his scornful dismissal of all other philosophical approaches to Ibsen:

> The desire to find some source other than Hegel is absurd. Ibsen professed his admiration for Hegel as he did for no other philosopher except, towards the end of his life, for Nietzsche.[9]

But this, as the New Critics used to say, is an extrinsic argument. It makes no difference in the end whether Ibsen liked Hegel and disliked Kierkegaard or the other way around; what counts is how much Hegel or Kierkegaard (or both) help us to analyze and interpret Ibsen. If Hegel's philosophy can illuminate Ibsen's plays, then Hegel should be used even if he had been writing on another planet; if not, then Hegel would not matter for critical purposes even if he and Ibsen had been Siamese twins.

Actually, a Hegelian approach *is* illuminating, as Johnston shows, but it also has its limitations. For one thing, there is Hegel's abstractness, his obsessive systematizing or "system building," that does not sit well with Ibsen's delight in the particular. When one thinks of little Ulf's cap in *Brand,* or the button-moulder's ladle (a souvenir from Ibsen's own childhood) in *Peer Gynt,* or Nora nibbling macaroons in *A Doll House,* or Osvald vomiting after smoking his father's pipe in *Ghosts,* or Dr. Stockmann ripping his pants at the town meeting in *An Enemy of the People,* one seems as far as possible from Hegel's grandiose abstractions, from Art and Religion and Philosophy, from the State and the World Spirit and so on. But more directly, there seems to be a distinct opposition between Hegel's love of the national State and Ibsen's hatred of it. Johnston points out, quite rightly, that Hegel did not set the State above the individual ultimately: "For

Hegel the highest realm of reality, above that of the State, was the realm of Art, Religion, and Philosophy—spiritual realities that transcended the State."[10] Nevertheless, for Hegel the State was still a very good thing, the highest social manifestation of the World Spirit, while in Ibsen's plays the State, whether conceived politically or socially, is almost always depicted as bad. Hegel's favorite play was Sophocles' *Antigone,* in which, at least as Hegel saw it, there is a balanced or "dialectical" struggle between the equally valid but opposing demands of the individual and of the State; but, except possibly in *The Pretenders,* Ibsen did not create struggles of that sort, usually weighting the scales heavily in favor of the individual.

All this does not mean that a Hegelian approach to Ibsen's drama is necessarily a barren one. It is just that *any* single philosophical system, when applied to a playwright as great as Ibsen, is going to prove inadequate. The Structuralist sees dramatic criticism as a heuristic process; we must constantly be revising our approaches and methods because of the infinitely complex nature of the task. Isolating one structure from the playtext automatically implies the downgrading of other structures, which must be exposed and developed later by other approaches. Criticism is thus endless.

Thus, I do not claim exclusivity for a Kierkegaardian approach to Ibsen; instead, I merely claim that such an approach may help to "point out what the reader might otherwise have missed," as T. S. Eliot once put it in a famous passage. Kierkegaard's philosophy provides insight into many aspects of Ibsen's plays, including elements that have often been considered obscurities or mistakes. Ibsen's technique of characterization is particularly Kierkegaardian, as are certain plot elements (the sudden transformations), as well as much of the symbolism. Even Ibsen's personal life often seems strangly to be derived from Kierkegaard; for example, Ibsen's attachments to young girls, late in his life, make him seem strikingly similar to the protagonist of Kierkegaard's "Diary of the Seducer." Nevertheless, it would be a mistake to press the Kierkegaardian approach to Ibsen too far. An Ibsen play is not a Kierkegaardian tract. The Structuralist distinction between code and message is crucial here; *the code is never the play itself,* but rather a means of enhancing our response to it. This distinction avoids all problems of whether the playwright's influences are conscious or unconscious, or even whether they are totally consistent with every element in his work. Interpretations of limited applicability are not necessarily worthless. In fact, the Kierkegaardian code often yields the most interesting results where, as in *An Enemy of the People,* Ibsen *deviates* from a strict adherence to Kierkegaardian philosophy.

Another code that I shall employ is the stylistic one of realism/Romanticism. There is nothing particularly new about dealing with Ibsen in these terms; critics have used one or the other in discussing his plays since they were first written. Recent critics have often gone so far as to suggest, as I shall, that the two styles are both to be found, simultaneously, in his middle, prose plays. The novelty will be that I shall be discussing these terms Structurally, rather than taxonomically. Realism/Romanticism is a stylistic code, rather than a two-part box for categorizing plays. As a code, understood intuitively by Ibsen and his audience, it generated certain strategies of playwriting, driving Ibsen to think in certain ways that would not have been possible using another code. This does not mean that it led Ibsen to a single, easily categorizable, inevitable style, as a taxonomic critic might conclude; on the contrary, Ibsen deviates from the traditional norms of this code at the same time that he is upholding it. As the Czech Structuralist Jan Mukařovský put it, a norm in literature "is in essence energy rather than a rule";[11] in good literary works "it tends to be violated rather than to be observed."[12] Thus Ibsen could at the same time be Romantic and realistic (though these terms are in many ways polar opposites), and, also at the same time, be uniquely himself.

Equally striking, I hope, will be the fact that I shall be treating realism/Romanticism in a nonmimetic way. Realism, in particular, has tended to be defined only as "closely imitating life," a definition that is vague and subjective when one tries to put it into practice. I have therefore devoted an entire chapter to Ibsen's realism, attempting to give it a precise, Structural definition that has nothing to do with "life" per se. The implications of this chapter reach beyond Ibsen's plays alone.

Finally, in interpreting Ibsen I shall be employing a theatrical code, dealing with such visual elements as settings, lighting, properties, and costumes. This does not mean that I intend to go into technical details of theatrical production, nor to tell anyone specifically how Ibsen must be performed. There is no single correct way of performing a playscript, just as there is no single correct critical approach to one. I shall instead be dealing with the *performance potential* of Ibsen's playscripts, the way that the scripts imply certain patterns of visual effect that, when realized in performance, can carry meaning. A given production could not, and need not attempt to, draw out all possible performance patterns; instead, directors can look upon a pattern as a source of inspiration, a line of potential to be explored.

Dealing with Ibsen in performance terms brings home his magnificent theatricality, which is meant in the deepest sense—not just his powerful characterizations or his well-known *coups de théâtre,* but also his mastery of time and space, his perfect control of every aspect of theatrical production. One becomes aware, if sensitive to Ibsen as a writer for the theater, that Nora in *A Doll House* must go through *three* doors to get outside at the end (the door she slams is the third one); her "doll house" is as confining as a prison. Or one discovers that it is raining *constantly* through the first three-quarters of *Ghosts,* which casts a special kind of gloom on all the dialogue and action. Or one responds to the power of the Mayor's hat and stick as they sit on a vacant chair in the printers' office in *An Enemy of the People*—a malevolent force overseeing all the characters' lives, even when it is not being talked about. A few critics, most notably John Northam, have touched on the theatrical elements in Ibsen, but rarely in much detail, and even more rarely in the Structuralist sense, in which performance structures convey ideas the way a language does.

Most critics have, in fact, treated Ibsen in purely literary terms, which can lead to serious errors of interpretation. Brian Johnston, for example, a critic whose orientation is narrowly literary, has maintained that "the openings of Ibsen's plays are almost always richer in small details than the condition of the endings,"[13] but no person who has ever dealt with Ibsen in the theater would make such a statement. The falling off in detail is an illusion brought on through only *reading* the scripts; naturally, Ibsen must establish the physical details of the play at the beginning, but they do not disappear merely because his stage directions or his characters stop mentioning them. Ibsen's control over such small detail rivals Shakespeare's. This was brought home to me in a production of *Ghosts* that I directed: during the famous scene in the first act in which Osvald enters smoking his father's pipe and recalls how his father had once forced him to smoke it as a child, his mother says, "Put the pipe down, dear. I don't want smoking in this room" (p. 221). He does so; and since the action is more or less continuous from there to the end of the play, and no one is ever called upon to remove the pipe, it *remains on the table* throughout the action, a physical "ghost" that is a constant reminder of the dead Captain Alving. But even that is only part of a larger pattern through which numerous objects accumulate in the room and are not removed. At the end of the play, the setting is thus filled with physical reminders of past events that the audience has seen: Regina's garden syringe (she has to put it down at the beginning of the play when Engstrand enters, and never has the opportunity to remove it), Mrs. Alving's books of "advanced" ideas, Osvald's cigar butt, the lamp that Regina brings in, the empty champagne bottles and glasses, the little box of morphine pills from Osvald's pocket. The past is thus tangibly present at the end of the play in a way that is both exciting and meaningful. Furthermore, this visual pattern is realizable in any production, whether on a proscenium or open stage, whether in a large theater or small, whether scrupulously realistic or highly distorted.

The three codes—the philosophical, the stylistic, and the theatrical—are all interrelated. The Kierkegaardian terminology, I shall suggest, provides the underlying "map" of the plays, and can be seen as the unifying principle. The other codes are like overlays on the basic map, which is why the Kierkegaardian terminology recurs with them. When geographers use overlays in this way, one can examine an individual overlay, and thus isolate a particular pattern in the terrain—say, of types of soil, or of vegetation, or of political boundaries—or one can lay on all at once, to appreciate the totality in all its complexity, and the relationships of the patterns to one another. But in the long run, the map, no matter how thoroughly overlaid, is only a guide to the terrain itself, and is not a substitute for it. One does not build a house on a map, but on solid earth. Similarly, my interpretation is meant to enhance the reader's appreciation of Ibsen's plays, and not, as in so much traditional criticism, provide a substitute for that experience. This book is not about me, but about Ibsen.

2/Ibsen's Allegorical Realism

IBSEN is interesting as a playwright who was equally capable in both Romantic and realistic styles. His early plays are extravagant, heroic, wide-ranging, and usually written in verse; his plays from *Pillars of Society* onward are subdued, have everyday characters, are narrowly focused, and are always written in prose. Even the late plays, in which critics have noted mythical and spiritual elements, still are written in a fundamentally realistic style. It is rare to find writers who are successful in both genres; of modern playwrights besides Ibsen, only Strindberg is another example.

The dichotomy in Ibsen's playwriting is not only an interesting technicality; it also goes to the heart of his method in the individual works. There is always a bit of the realistic operating in his early Romantic plays; and there is always a good deal of the Romantic operating in his realistic plays. As John Northam has argued,

> The modern prose plays by which Ibsen is best known amongst foreigners are, for him, the fusion he had been searching for between form and vision: fully dramatic representations of modern life that are also capable of expressing his sense of the heroic potential that exists even in modern man.[1]

Or, as G. Wilson Knight put it, "Beneath [Ibsen's] modern trappings stalk heroism and grandeur."[2] The thesis of this book is that there is an allegorical substructure to Ibsen's

33

realism in the social plays as well as in the more obvious examples like *Rosmersholm, Hedda Gabler,* or *The Master Builder,* and furthermore that this substructure has a more distinct and pervasive nature than has previously been realized. *A Doll House, Ghosts,* and *An Enemy of the People* can be called, very precisely, examples of an "allegorical realism."

Before we can understand this phrase, however, it is necessary to explore the meanings of terms like *realism* and *Romanticism* as applied to drama. *Realism* in particular is one of those words that are tossed about casually as if requiring no definition. Everyone connected with the theater knows what realism means: it is just the reflection of real life, presented on the stage. Such a definition seems suitably bland and straightforward, but it leaves a lot that is unexplained. Why, for example, if the early realistic playwrights were only concerned with the neutral, passive reflection of life, were they often denounced as subversives or as purveyors of filth? Why, conversely, do modern plays that literally present actual events from life—the so-called Theatre of Fact—seem so *un*realistic? Plays in this genre reflect life far more exactly than the early realists ever dreamed of doing, yet they seem abstract, detached, and unrevealing, more like the Epic drama of Bertolt Brecht than anything by Zola or Brieux or Ibsen. Peter Weiss's *The Investigation,* for example, takes literally every word of its dialogue from the transcript of a Nazi war-crime trial—yet it is set completely in verse!

All this suggests that there is something characteristic about the content of nineteenth-century realistic drama that is separate from the external form. The early realistic playwrights were not just concerned with presenting real life on stage as a technical exercise; if they had been, they would have anticipated Weiss, Hochhuth, and Bentley, and used actual people for their characters, speaking their real-life words. But this never happened. The nineteenth-century realists were not after reality *in toto,* nor even life taken at random, but rather were aiming to show those particular aspects of life that their hypocritical bourgeois society was trying to cover up. This is why the playwrights—particularly the more extreme realists like Zola, Becque, or Hauptmann, often referred to as "naturalists"—liked to depict or describe murder, rape, adultery, greed, brutality, illegitimacy, squalor, and class conflict. It was not so much from a love of the sordid, as their opponents maintained, but rather from a hatred of hypocrisy. Nineteenth-century realistic drama was "scientific," not in the pure sense of being detached and observing, but in the applied sense of wanting to diagnose a patient and restore him to health. The playwrights typically compared themselves not to chemists or physicists or biologists, but rather to doctors. (Indeed, some, like Chekhov, *were* doctors, and Ibsen himself at one time considered a medical career.) Realistic content in nineteenth-century drama is thus, in a word, *disease.*

Nevertheless, even this concept comes up against difficulties in twentieth-century theater. There are plenty of modern plays that are nonrealistic or even loudly *anti*realistic, whose content is as sordid as any of those of the realists or naturalists. Brecht's Epic dramas have homosexuality, castration, military atrocity, and a man who falls into a machine in a meat-packing company and is turned into bacon (an incident borrowed from Upton Sinclair's naturalistic novel, *The Jungle*). More recently, the hortatory performances of the Living Theatre, which completely lacked the realistic matrices of plot, setting, and character, have included drug-taking, nudity, and simulated sex. All this suggests that there are two senses in which the word *realistic* is used, one referring to form and the other to content. The word actually requires two definitions, one external and the other internal. Plays of the "Theatre of Fact" are internally realistic because they depict real people and actual events, while plays like those of Brecht or the Living Theatre also have an internal realism (or "naturalism") in the sense of depicting the sordid, the corrupt, the physical. But such works are not realistic in an *external* sense, which is why they do not *seem* realistic to us, at least not in the ways that the works of Zola, Ibsen, Strindberg, or Chekhov seem realistic. In other words, verisimilitude (the feeling that a play is lifelike) and the depiction of literal reality are two separate things.

If the internal definition of realism is either "actuality," in a very strict sense, or alternatively "disease," in a very broad sense, what is the external definition? What is wanted here is not a definition in mimetic terms that will describe how much or what kind of reality is represented, but rather a definition in technical terms that will describe the means of representation. Mimetic definitions are really internal, applicable to content but telling us nothing about form. An external definition that is suitably technical can be derived from the ideas in Erich Auerbach's book, *Mimesis*, a profound work that has had far too little influence on dramatic criticism. Auerbach sees two basic styles in all of Western literature, as exemplified by Homer on the one extreme, and the stories of the Old Testament on the other. The Homeric style, according to Auerbach, attempts the following:

> To represent phenomena in a fully externalized form, visible and palpable in all their parts, and completely fixed in their spatial and temporal relations. Nor do psychological processes receive any other treatment: here too nothing must remain hidden and unexpressed.... A continuous rhythmic procession of phenomena passes by, and never is there a form left fragmentary or half-illuminated, never a lacuna, never a gap, never a glimpse of unplumbed depths.[3]

The Old Testament style, on the other hand, has totally contrasting techniques:

> Certain parts brought into high relief, others left obscure, abruptness, suggestive influence of the unexpressed, "background" quality, multiplicity of meanings and the need for interpretation, universal-historical claims, development of the concept of the historically becoming, and preoccupation with the problematic.[4]

In the former case, the organizing principle is *in* the work, making it self-contained, flowing, linearly connected; in the latter case, the organizing principle lies *behind* the work as God's mysterious and difficult plan of history, making the surface events isolated from one another, full of abrupt and unexplained changes, and connected only thematically or "spatially." The Homeric style is *continuous,* the Biblical style *discontinuous.*

Note that these are nonmimetic definitions. They say nothing about the reality of what is represented, but only about the manner in which the representation takes place. Ironically, the continuous Homeric style *seems* more real than the discontinuous Biblical style, at least at the time of reading, even though much of what Homer describes, such as the exploits of gods and legendary heroes, is fictitious. This is because the purpose of his flowing style is, in Auerbach's words, "to bewitch the senses."[5] The Bible seems less real, not in a scientific sense, because it is presumably about real events and people, but in the sense of verisimilitude. That is, while reading the Bible one has little feeling that "this is happening here and now," because one is not being "bewitched" as with Homer but rather being taught a lesson. In Brechtian terms, the abrupt shifts and discontinuities in the Bible stories are an "alienation effect" that prevents us from being carried away, forcing us instead to ponder the stories' deeper significance.

Here too is the explanation for why plays from the Epic Theatre or the Theatre of Fact lack a feeling of verisimilitude despite their shocking and often literally real subject matter. A play like Weiss's *The Investigation,* though taken point-blank from life, is full of discontinuities that interrupt the flow of the play and prevent us from becoming involved. The setting of the dialogue in verse is a discontinuity in itself; what might have flowed smoothly has been broken into uneven lines. But even more important in the play's alienation effects is what the script leaves out. The characters, for example, lack the personal backgrounds that we have come to expect in a realistic play. Strindberg, for example, wrote the following in his Preface to *Miss Julie* about the title character:

> I see Miss Julie's tragic fate to be the result of many circumstances: the mother's character, the father's mistaken upbringing of the girl, her own nature, and the influence of her fiancé on a weak, degenerate mind. Also, more directly, the festive mood of Midsummer Eve, her father's absence, her monthly indisposition, her pre-occupation with animals, the excitement of dancing, the magic of dusk, the strongly aphrodisiac influence of flowers, and finally the chance that drives the couple into a room alone—to which must be added the urgency of the excited man.[6]

Strindberg actually puts all this background information into the playscript as well, including the detail about Miss Julie's menstrual period. But in Weiss's script, most such personal material remains "hidden and unexpressed," to use Auerbach's words, because in real life people rarely expose the stories of their childhood, their families, their daily work, their health, their philosophies of life, their hopes and fears and anxieties—at least, not in the few hours that are available to the playwright for a performance. Thus Weiss's characters, though real, tend to become reduced to a judge, a medical orderly, an S.S. corporal, a prosecuting attorney, and so on—one-dimensional types that are almost allegorical. The audience is forced to plumb the depths of the characters for themselves, to work out what might have motivated the real-life people behind them. Instead of a "continuous rhythmic procession of phenomena," the audience gets a disjointed series of characters and stories that requires, as with the Bible, a constant active involvement to work out a pattern behind the disconnected surface.

Nineteenth-century dramatic realism, on the other hand, was written in the Homeric style, with "never a lacuna, never a gap, never a glimpse of unplumbed depths." All was flowing and continuous. Consider the following passage, from the opening of *Ghosts:*

> REGINA *(in a low voice).* What do you want? Just stay where you are. Why, you're dripping wet.
> ENGSTRAND. It's God's own rain, my girl.
> REGINA. The devil's rain, it is!
> ENGSTRAND. Jeez, how you talk, Regina. *(Hobbles a few steps into the room.)* But now, what I wanted to say—
> REGINA. Stop stomping about with that foot, will you! The young master's sleeping upstairs.
> ENGSTRAND. Still sleeping? In broad daylight?
> REGINA. That's none of your business.
> ENGSTRAND. I was out on a binge last night—
> REGINA. I can imagine.
> ENGSTRAND. Yes, because we mortals are weak, my girl—
> REGINA. Yes, so we are. (Pp. 203-4)

Rain is mentioned in the first three speeches, providing a connecting link; Regina brings it up (thus connecting the dialogue to the setting), causing Engstrand to respond, which causes Regina to respond in turn. Throughout the passage, each character's speech stimulates the next; sometimes they even overlap each other, adding to the sense of continuous flow. From formally written plays, like those of Shakespeare, one can extract the speeches of a single character, such as Macbeth, and have a perfectly meaningful collection of poems, epigrams, and dissertations; a similar collection of Regina's speeches from *Ghosts* would make no sense at all. Bartlett's *Familiar Quotations* is full of examples from Shakespeare, but has few from Ibsen, not because Ibsen's plays are inferior, but rather because any speeches in them that might have stood out as set pieces have been rewritten. (Actually, Ibsen's prose plays do contain, on occasion, recognizable set speeches, but this is precisely where the plays seem unnaturalistic.) Shakespeare thinks in terms of the fixed character and the set speech, being notoriously careless about the connecting details like Iago's motivation or Lady Macbeth's children; Ibsen in his realistic plays is thinking in terms of the continuing dialogue, as well as connections between character and motivation, character and character, and dialogue and setting.

Continuity, or direct connectedness, is thus the unifying principle for dramatic realism in the external sense. An externally realistic play has no gaps; it also, like a continuous line, has no recognizable beginnings or ends either. Thus, within a realistic setting, unlike, say, the medieval "mansion" style where little houses representing heaven, hell, Jerusalem, Rome, and so on were scattered about the stage, there can be no neutral ground that stands for no place in particular. If there are a door and a window there must be a wall in between; it is not enough to plunk them down like two "mansions," and let the intervening space take care of itself. But furthermore, a realistic setting may not end abruptly at the sides or back of the stage; if there is a door, there must be a hall behind it, and then perhaps a stairway, and another door, and then a street outside, and so on. If the audience cannot see all of this, then they must at least be made to sense its presence; a character must seem to enter *from* somewhere and exit *to* somewhere. Ibsen's Engstrand enters the room in the scene above literally bringing some of the rain and mist in with him. Regina carries "an empty garden-syringe in her hand," which shows where she has been also. The scene is full of talk about important nearby places we cannot see, or can see only part of: the garden, Osvald's bedroom, the kitchen, the orphanage, the fjord, the town, the schoolhouse, Engstrand's proposed sailors' home "in Little Harbor Street." And when Engstrand leaves, it is not just an "exit off," but a departure specifically "down the kitchen stairs," which we cannot see. Nonrealistic drama may of course contain mentionings of offstage places, but they are not developed so elaborately, nor connected so carefully and incessantly to the onstage dialogue and action.

The "no gaps, no ends" principle applies to time as well as to space. Extreme examples of plot continuity occur in plays like Strindberg's *Miss Julie,* where the traditional Unity of Time is followed to the letter, with no scene breaks or intermissions despite the fact that it is almost as long as an ordinary three-act play; the time depicted is thus exactly the same as performance time. But even when not strictly continuous, nineteenth-century realistic plays have generally fewer acts and fewer scenes than does previous drama. Thus Ibsen's *Peer Gynt,* written in the Romantic style, has five acts and 38 scenes, depicting numerous events in the lifetime of the title character from early youth to extreme old age; *Ghosts,* on the other hand, while having many similarities to *Peer Gynt* (which I shall be discussing later), has only three acts, each consisting of a single scene, and covers a total period of less than one day. While the intermissions in *Ghosts* do represent gaps in time, the dialogue at the beginning of the second and third acts fills in for the audience what took place during the intervals: Act 2 begins with Manders's complimenting Mrs. Alving on the meal they have just eaten, while the very first line of Act 3 refers to the orphanage, which had caught fire at the end of the previous act, as having just burned to the ground. The continuous flow of action beguiles us into thinking that we are actually watching a real event.

As a matter of fact, the time scheme of *Ghosts,* when examined with detachment, turns out to be impossible. The play begins around late morning. It cannot be much earlier, because Engstrand expresses great surprise that Osvald is still asleep, "in broad daylight" (p. 203), long after everyone else is up and busy. Nor can it be much later, for Engstrand says, "This afternoon I'll be done with my work down at the schoolhouse" (p. 204). At the end of the first act, the meal about to be eaten is referred to as "lunch." (The word is less specific in the Norwegian, and might refer to dinner, but the fact that the meal takes place while it is still light makes Fjelde's translation a reasonable one.) Act 2 begins immediately after the meal, yet less than half an hour along it is twilight, and Mrs. Alving has to call for a lamp. Assuming a very slow lunch, and an early sunset (accurate for Norway if it is wintertime), this places the end of Act 2 at about four o'clock in the afternoon. The only thing that happens in the intermission is that the orphanage, which began burning at the end of Act 2, burns down; at the beginning of Act 3, in fact, "it's burning still in the basement" (p. 260). It appears to have burned very quickly, since there was no chance to save it, but assuming that it was a *very large* orphanage (we never hear many specifics about it), it might have taken it two or three hours to be consumed. This places the beginning of Act 3 at about seven o'clock—say, eight o'clock at the very outside. Since Act 3 runs only about half an hour, this means that the famous sunrise at the end of the play takes place at 8:30 in the evening!

The point is, of course, that because of the continuity of

the action, the audience never notices any mistake. Time is everywhere condensed in the play, rather than anywhere suddenly altered, so that the audience does not realize that the play's "clock" is running about three times as fast as a normal one. This discrepancy shows, again, that there is a difference between external and internal realism; it is quite possible to have a play that *seems* real despite certain elements that are utterly impossible.

In addition to being continuous during its playing time, the plot of a realistic play extends continuously backward and forward. Just as the setting flows offstage with no definite boundaries, so too the plot has no decisive beginning or ending. It is well known that realistic playwrights typically used lengthy exposition to convince the audience that what they see is merely the continuation of a long story; what is less well recognized is the playwrights' corresponding tendency to plant seeds in the play to convince the audience that the action will continue even after the final curtain. The story in Ibsen's *Ghosts* extends back over thirty years; we learn about Mrs. Alving's upbringing, her marriage, her husband's character (ostensible and actual), her rearing of Osvald, her relationship with Manders, and her management of the estate since her husband's death—all before the play is half over. And at the end, we know that Engstrand will build his Sailors' Home with the aid of Pastor Manders, that Regina will "go to her ruin" as a prostitute, and that Mrs. Alving will have to keep up her façade of respectability. Most important, our interest is focused, as the curtain falls, on the question of whether Mrs. Alving will commit euthanasia, giving Osvald the morphine pills he has begged her for. Where the dialogue in the first act was generally written in the past tense, that in the last act is written in the future. There has been a gradual shift from an obsession with what did happen to an obsession with what will happen.

In both space and time, then, *Ghosts* maintains for the

audience a continuous façade. Nineteenth-century audiences accepted this style as "real" because it conformed to their notion of how the world functioned. Influenced by the spectacular rise of science and technology, they had come to see the world as a mechanical system that was coherent, comprehensible, and self-contained. Everything in life was connected only to life; that is, every event could be explained in terms of other such events, rather than in terms of gods, demons, fairies, "a divine plan," "the chain of being," "God's mysterious will," and so on. Causality was always *in* the world rather than somewhere behind it. This was a reason for realistic content in literature as well: a belief in a world that is ultimately only physical caused writers inevitably to deal with subject matter that was material, fleshly, anti-ideal. In a more typical realistic play than *Ghosts,* such as one by Zola or Brieux, there is a unifying principle behind both the form and the content that can be summed up by the phrase *scientific determinism.* The form of the plays is continuous, rolling along without a hitch like a well-oiled machine; similarly, the characters and events are controlled by mechanistic forces like sexual desire, hunger, or greed, in continuous harmony with their environment even when they appear to be suffering. All is explicable, psychological (in the behaviorist sense), inevitable. "Nothing must remain hidden or unexpressed."

With Ibsen, however, there is *not* this simple harmony between content and form, the inner and the outer kinds of realism. Recognition of this fact is essential for the proper understanding of his social drama. *A Doll House, Ghosts,* and *An Enemy of the People* are realistic in the external sense, but definitely not so in the internal sense, where they maintain the convention of Ibsen's earlier Romantic style. Ibsen is thus a mirror opposite to modern writers like Brecht: where Brecht wrote plays that were externally discontinuous (i.e., conventionalized, alienated, "Epic"), but internally continuous (i.e., determined, fleshly, anti-idealistic), Ibsen wrote his social plays to be externally continuous (i.e., unbroken, flowing, beguiling) but internally discontinuous (i.e., undetermined, allegorical, idealized).

This incongruity may at first seem strange. A smooth, machinelike external framework in a play normally ought to imply characters who are controlled by that framework, rather than characters who are independent, allegorical types. But the best works of art are not "normal." There is something about a play that is both internally and externally realistic, such as Strindberg's *Miss Julie,* that is simply too smooth, too obvious, too clear. We know too much about Miss Julie. In life, a universal quality of my knowledge of another person is the sense of a background beyond my understanding, of a human being as complex and incomprehensible as I am myself. Yet there Miss Julie stands on the stage, completely explained, completely understood. It is all a matter of flowers, twilight, menstruation. Although in one way she is very lifelike, in a more important way she is lif*eless,* being more a scientific case study than a recognizable human being. This was the sort of problem with realistic drama that Artaud was pointing to when he complained that "Psychology, which works relentlessly to reduce the unknown to the known, to the quotidian and the ordinary, is the cause of the theatre's abasement and its fearful loss of energy."[7] Ibsen is a better realistic writer than Strindberg because he never falls into this trap. Ibsen's characters can never be explained away as Strindberg's Miss Julie can. There is thus a kind of counterpoint between Ibsen's content and form in the social plays; the material is always threatening to burst out of its prescribed conventions. Ibsen's social plays do not merely take over unaltered the scientific world view; Ibsen realized that science does *not* have all the answers, no matter how much it may dominate our consciousness.

As I shall try to show, Ibsen's characters are primarily types, rather than realistically motivated complexes, and his principal characters are defined by free choice, rather than being controlled by internal or external forces. Yet in his social plays Ibsen maintains, as much as possible, the external façade of realism. This sets up an essential ambiguity: his principal characters at times seem to be controlled, as by a male-chauvinist society in *A Doll House*, hypocritical morality in *Ghosts*, or greed in *An Enemy of the People*, yet at bottom they are depicted as free. This paradox is the very thing that makes the plays interesting, that prevents them from being "quotidian and ordinary." As a matter of fact, science has *not* resolved the old philosophical debate on free will versus determinism, which is what makes this problem still so fruitful artistically. We hear every day arguments over whether criminals are innocent victims of their impoverished backgrounds or wicked people who should be punished for the evil life they have freely chosen. We wonder whether the Vietnam war or the Watergate scandals were the result of some inadequacy in our social system, or of a few capricious individuals abusing their power. I believe that there is no simple answer to these questions, which is the very thing that makes them fascinating. If there were a simple answer to the question of free will or determinism, good playwrights would not write about it, for art is concerned with precisely those areas of human experience where there is no clear, logical solution.

Ambiguity, that favorite concept of the New Critics (along with variations like "paradox," "complexity," and "irony"), has never been widely accepted by critics of drama, nor by theater practitioners. The idea that a play might mean two (or more) things at once, or even two *opposing* things, is generally greeted with amazement or scorn. Playwrights like Ibsen are supposed to have a few important but simple ideas, which they proceed to transform into stage terms in a straightforward way. *A Doll House* advocates women's rights, *Ghosts* attacks social hypocrisy, *An Enemy of the People* champions scientific progress. The acceptance of these plays was at first enhanced by these simplistic ideas about them, but later, as the issues faded in popularity, the plays' reputations suffered accordingly. If we had seen these plays from the beginning for what they are—complex treatments of modern life, in which allegorical characters are placed in a scientific and technological framework—they would have received less notoriety at first, but would have sustained interest longer. But this would have required an acceptance of ambiguity as a structural principle in Ibsen's drama, which may be difficult even today. Even Auerbach's view of the continuous mode in literature, brilliant though it is, implies that no "third dimension" is possible: "Nothing must remain hidden and unexpressed . . . never a glimpse of unplumbed depths." The paradox with Ibsen is that nothing appears to be hidden, yet actually a good deal is hidden; the form of the social plays never *forces* us to glimpse unplumbed depths, as the Bible does, but those depths are there nonetheless.

Ibsen's plays, then, are never single; they contain elements that are double and even multiple, and the elements are often paradoxical and contradictory—impossible in terms of ordinary logic, and hence impossible in terms of traditional dramatic criticism. Such criticism has generally been too polarized—either Ibsen was a social critic, or he was a poet, but not both. But we should reject the original view of "Ibsen the pamphleteer," *not* because it elevated his social plays above his "mythic" ones, but rather because it was an oversimplification of all Ibsen's plays, *including* the social ones.

Consider the issue of symbolic or "mythic" patterns in Ibsen's drama. Orley Holtan's position is fairly typical:

> In [the social] plays the mythic pattern is thoroughly displaced in the direction of realism. . . . The symbolism of the plays is rather confined. The symbols used (Nora's Tarantella, the "ghosts," the diseased baths) have fairly direct and tangible referents. There is little of the quicksilver quality of the wild duck or the white horses and little sense of mystery that cannot be psychologically or sociologically explained. In short, even though mythic patterns can be discerned in those plays, myth has been so thoroughly displaced as almost to disappear completely.[8]

This is just the kind of exclusivist thinking that is dangerous with Ibsen. His late plays are symbolic—so his social plays cannot be, or at least not very greatly. Now it is true that the symbolism in Ibsen's late plays is of a different type from that in the middle ones. In the late plays, Ibsen not only strains the realistic façade, he actually breaks it. Symbols like the wild duck or the white horses seem to stand out from the fabric of the play, unjustified and unmotivated. The wild duck is striking as a symbol, connoting mystery, escapism, death, Hedvig's conflicting emotions, Hedvig herself, and so on. Its referents are multiple, reaching into the obscure, but there is no doubt that the duck *is* a symbol. In terms of the play's action, in fact, it seems silly or bizarre. What a strange thing for these people to be playing with, we think. And we never even see it! The duck could almost be written out of the play as it stands, or changed into something else more suitable for a family pet, like a dog or a canary. The wild duck really is a discontinuous element of the play, forcing us to consider it as a thing apart, and leading us to "a glimpse of unplumbed depths." But this does not necessarily make it more symbolic, in the sense of having a wider or deeper range of connotations than a more integrated symbol. It is just more obvious, requiring less effort on the audience's part to respond to it in a symbolic way.

Consider, by contrast, a symbol like the lamp that is brought on in the second act of *Ghosts*. Unlike the wild duck, it is thoroughly justified in realistic terms: the play takes place in a house, and nineteenth-century houses used oil lamps. Regina brings the lamp in because it is getting dark, and also because it is her job as a servant to do so. The lamp is thus completely integrated into the façade of the play, with direct, continuous connections in space and time with other objects, events, and characters. But the lamp is also symbolic, and not just in "direct and tangible" ways: it evokes indirect associations in the sensitive observer's mind that leap across the direct, linear relationships. It suggests Osvald's disease, with which he is "burning up." It recalls Captain Alving's pipe, which is still onstage when the lamp is brought in. Its light is soon amplified by that from the burning orphanage offstage. It is turned off at the end of the play, to be replaced by the morning sunlight breaking through the mist, at the moment Osvald's madness breaks out. Finally, the lamp suggests Regina herself, who brings it in, and "the glow of her health," which is supposed to restore Osvald in the same way that the lamp dispels the gloom. Ultimately, as I shall attempt to show in the chapter on *Ghosts*, light in the play reaches beyond even these earthly associations, suggesting the force of life, yet ironically also the force of death and destruction. It illuminates, clarifies, warms, sustains—yet it also sickens, burns, destroys. Thus, for all the realistic justification for the lamp, it is just as evocative a symbol as the wild duck; though it is more subtle, it is ultimately no less powerful.

Dramatic realism, then, is something considerably more flexible than is commonly supposed. To say that a play is realistic is really a neutral observation, like saying that a play is written in blank verse. The important thing is to determine what a playwright like Ibsen *does* with the realistic conventions. T. S. Eliot once pointed out that the invention of blank verse in Elizabethan times "may be likened to the analysis of that astonishing industrial product coal tar. Marlowe's verse is one of the earlier derivatives, but it possesses properties which are not repeated in any of the analytic or synthetic blank verses discovered somewhat later."[9] Thus, Marlowe's blank verse was different from Shakespeare's, Shakespeare's from Jonson's, and so on. The innovation of realism in the late nineteenth-century theater made possible a similarly wide number of derivatives. Ibsen's realism is different from Strindberg's, deeper, more allegorical or symbolic, more mythic; similarly, Strindberg's realism is different from Hauptmann's, and Hauptmann's from Chekhov's. There is good realism and bad realism, comic and tragic, subtle and blatant, highbrow and low.

We might consider the amazing durability of dramatic realism, whose demise was predicted almost from its inception. Copying life directly was considered to be a limited gimmick that could never last. Yet playwrights like Chekhov, O'Casey, and O'Neill achieved their greatest successes with realism, while generally failing when they attempted various kinds of formalism. Even today, when we are besieged with theories about "pure" or "nonmatrixed" theater, we find realism thriving with playwrights like David Storey, Ed Bullins, or Michel Tremblay. Harold Pinter, weird though his plays may be, operates through the continuity technique of realism. All this is possible because realism does *not* necessarily imply an inner content that is mechanistic and inhuman; such an approach is merely one of two broad strategies that the realistic playwright can employ. Failure to recognize this is the basis for much of the prejudice that has long been directed against realism in the theater. Yeats, for example, was simply incapable of responding to the symbolism and allegory in Ibsen's social plays:

> I hated the play [*A Doll House*]; what was it but Carolus Duran, Bastien-Lepage, Huxley and Tyndall all over again? I resented being invited to admire dialogue so close to modern educated speech that music and style were impossible . . . as time passed Ibsen became in my eyes the chosen author of very clever young journalists, who, condemned to their treadmill of abstraction, hated music and style.[10]

For Yeats, then, continuous façade drawn from everyday life automatically implied an inner content that was mundane and journalistic. But it is interesting to compare Yeats's own formal poetic dramas with the realistic plays of his more successful protégés, Synge and O'Casey. Synge, in particular, recognized what James Joyce had tried to point out to Yeats, that it was possible and even appropriate to employ the new realistic style "in depth," that the rattling teacups and the simple chitchat of ordinary people could resonate with additional meanings that were deeply allegorical. *Playboy of the Western World* became more popular in the theater than Yeats's plays, not because it was better written, but rather because it employed a style that was immediately accessible to an audience having a materialistic, technological orientation, while Yeats's fondness for the archaic or foreign created an inevitable barrier for them. *Playboy* actually does what Yeats wanted drama to do, namely, unify the ideal and the real, but it does it the other way round from the way Yeats thought was necessary, by putting idealized content into a realistic frame rather than realistic content into an idealized frame.

Ibsen's social plays operate like *Playboy of the Western World,* and indeed provided the models for it. They are tense and exciting rather than witty and charming, but like *Playboy* they present a surface that is continuous and "beguiling," but that hides undercurrents of profundity. It may be difficult to accept this paradox for plays whose reputation is one of blunt straightforwardness, but that is a reputation I hope to dispel.

3/*Brand* and *Peer Gynt:* Ibsen's *Either/Or*

BEFORE examining Ibsen's social plays in detail, I should like to look first at the two best plays of his initial, Romantic period: *Brand* and *Peer Gynt.* Of these, John Northam has written:

> *Brand* (1866) and *Peer Gynt* (1867) are usually taken to represent the climax of Ibsen's earlier and more truly poetical period. They can also be seen as decisive stages in the clarification of one of his twin problems, that of defining for himself what modern heroism would amount to. Ibsen deliberately avoids the other problem of dramatic form by writing these works not as plays for performance but as dramatic poems. . . . He used his freedom not just to write his greatest poetry, in the formal sense, but to give his fullest versions of the obverse and reverse sides of the one thing that fascinated him continuously. *Brand* is a study of the heroic; *Peer Gynt* of the unheroic in the recognizably modern world; these dramatic poems represent the furthest penetration so far of Ibsen's imagination into that complex of tensions.[1]

Thus, Ibsen's allegorical patterns can be seen in pure form in these plays, making them invaluable for studying the later ones where the allegorical content, as I have already suggested, is disguised by the realistic façade. *Brand* and *Peer Gynt* are prototypes; while it would be too crude to say that Ibsen merely went on to write these plays over again, such a statement is closer to the truth than the idea that the social plays stand out like a sore thumb. As Northam points out, *Brand* and *Peer Gynt* were written as "closet dramas," or plays meant only to be read (although they have occasionally been staged, and usually with success), in order that Ibsen might temporarily free himself from the rigors of the practical theater; in the realistic plays that were to follow, Ibsen found the dramatic form he had been searching for, subjecting the same inner content to its exacting requirements. One finds in the realistic social plays the same character types, ideas, motifs, movements, and conflicts as in *Brand* and *Peer Gynt*, although the emphases are constantly shifting.

Both *Brand* and *Peer Gynt* are long, extravagant plays written in typical Romantic style. They are in verse, have many changes of scene and jumps in time, involve spectacular scenic effects (some of which, like an avalanche and a shipwreck, are impossible to stage illusionistically, since Ibsen was not writing for the theater), and focus on a single hero. Both are concerned with the problems of the individual, with the rest of society seen as an adversary, or as a temptation. The modern, sociological notion that the individual is merely a pawn of sociological and historical forces is not in evidence. Even Peer Gynt, who always drifts with the tide, is shown as having *alternatives*—he should have remained with his devoted lover, Solveig, for example, instead of traveling around the world. Other characters are specifically contrasted with Peer, such as the boy who cuts off his finger to avoid being drafted, or Solveig herself, who is eternally faithful, in order to show that other kinds of behavior are possible.

Nor can the individuals in *Brand* and *Peer Gynt* be considered as the products of forces within. Of course, it is always possible to speculate about what drives a character in a play, but characters should not really be called "psychological" unless the play itself, directly or indirectly, provides us with this background information. These plays provide none. The title character of each is a fixed type rather than the "soul-complex" that Strindberg, for example, was later to demand. We learn next to nothing about Brand's or Peer's preconditionings, childhood traumas, sexual awakenings, and the like. Instead, Brand is simply characterized as a fanatic (of a very special and interesting kind, to be sure), while Peer is his exact opposite—a drifter and wastrel. Both were hailed at the time of their first appearance as "typical" Norwegian characters, the former embodying everything Norwegians wanted to be (but usually failed to achieve), and the latter embodying everything they wanted to avoid (but usually ended up becoming).[2] Nowadays, after a century of realistic literature, many critics would find such an approach to characterization narrow or even bigoted. But static character types were typical in the drama of the period, as well as in previous drama, and Ibsen himself never completely escaped using them.

Brand is a play about a small-town preacher. One almost forgets this fact in reading the play, because he is such a spectacular character—too great for his surroundings, as some of the other characters even remark. He springs full-blown into the first scene, and remains on stage throughout almost the entire long play. Although he apparently grew up in the small Norwegian coastal town in which the play is set—his mother is one of the town's inhabitants, and there are occasional references in the script to Brand's boyhood—we are given none of the elaborate personal background that would be expected in a realistic play. Brand has been an itinerant preacher when the play begins, and is passing through his home town, where he takes the inhabitants completely by surprise through the power of his will and the sternness of his demands.

There is an obvious parallel to Jesus' mission to Galilee in the New Testament. In fact there are numerous times in the play when Brand is compared to Christ, the most striking occurring in the last act, in a scene with Gerd, a strange, wild girl who lives in the mountains. Brand has failed in his attempt to lead his parishioners to a spectacular "ice church" high in the mountains, and is discovered by Gerd alone and exhausted on the mountainside. She examines his hands and discovers stigmata:

> They're scarred with nails. There's blood in your hair.
> The thorn's teeth have cut your forehead.
> You've been on the cross.
>
> (P. 155)

Auerbach, in *Mimesis,* identified the discontinuous style of works like *Brand* with the Bible, and there is an unquestionable biblical influence on the play. The connection should not be pushed to the point of literal identification, however. Brand is far different from the "gentle Jesus, meek and mild" of tradition. He resembles more the stern God of the Old Testament, or perhaps even a war god of Norse myth, exhorting his followers to self-sacrifice and total, even blind, dedication to the ideal. As he himself says at one point, "I hardly know if I'm a Christian" (p. 60). There are few direct references to Scripture in the play, and no traditional theology. Brand has only contempt for the joyous aspects of Christianity, with its belief in personal redemption through Christ's sacrifice. This attitude, he feels, lets man off the hook too easily; it is a form of escapism, focusing man's attention on the hereafter instead of the awesome challenges that life presents in this world. Thus Brand becomes not an evangelist, preaching redemption through faith, but rather a kind of secular priest, preaching personal fulfillment through total commitment.

Brand is particularly contemptuous of pettiness, compromise, or hypocrisy, taking the phrase "All or Nothing" as his motto. Each act is a confrontation with a different person or group: In the first act Brand, traveling through the mountains, meets Ejnar, a painter, and Agnes, his fiancée; Brand denounces them for their amoral sensualism and naive religion:

> All you want is to flirt
> And play, and laugh; to do lip service to your faith
> But not to know the truth; to leave your suffering
> To someone who they say died for your sake.
> He died for you, so you are free to dance.
> To dance, yes; but whither?
>
> (P. 59)

In the second act, Brand descends to the fjord and finds the villagers struggling to get food being doled out by the Mayor. The villagers are characterized throughout as greedy, self-serving, yet unconsciously hypocritical, paying lip service to their faith like Ejnar and Agnes. The Mayor himself is an interesting character who is also a hypocrite, but whose hypocrisy is wholly conscious, as he cynically manipulates the villagers. The pattern of the unconscious versus the conscious hypocrite is one that Ibsen will repeat in the social plays; while neither type is shown to be exactly admirable, Ibsen usually implies that the conscious hypocrite is somehow better, that it is worse to fool oneself than to fool others. The villagers' mindless insincerity is disgusting, but there is a certain charm to the Mayor's open cynicism:

> MAYOR. You must take a quarter less than you had last time.
> You've one less mouth to feed.
> SECOND MAN. Yes, Ragnhild died yesterday.
> MAYOR, *makes a note.* One less. Well, a saving's a saving.
>
> (P. 70)

The villagers become incensed by Brand's challenges, shouting to have him driven out of the village or even killed. This is Ibsen at his most antidemocratic, foreshadowing *An Enemy of the People,* where angry, self-serving villagers also attack the hero for telling the truth. Just as the scene approaches catastrophe, a distraught woman enters, screaming for a priest; her husband, in a fit of madness, killed their starving child, and now lives in terror of dying unshriven. Brand immediately offers to go to his aid, but the man lives across the stormy fjord, and of course none of the cowardly villagers is willing to ferry Brand across, although a boat is available. It is interesting that Brand, who does not seem to believe in redemption, would be so eager to go to shrive someone; the incident shows how Brand is driven by a passion for duty for its own sake, rather than for any external benefit.

Then abruptly an event occurs that is repeated dozens of times in Ibsen's later work: the sudden transformation of an individual. Agnes steps forward, denouncing her former hedonistic way of life, and agrees to cross the fjord with Brand. Her words to her former fiancé are significant—"All God's ocean lies between us now" (p. 74). Her transformation is sudden, spontaneous, and immense. Echoes of this phrase are repeated in crucial moments in Ibsen's later plays, as when Helmer in the final scene of *A Doll House* cries out in horror to Nora that "There's a gulf that's opened between us" (p. 195). A crevasse literally separated Brand from Agnes and Ejnar in the scene in the mountains in Act 1. In the final Act, after Agnes's death, her spirit appears to Brand in the mountains. When he moves toward her, she screams "Stop! A gulf lies between us" (p. 151), and later expands this physical fact into a metaphor:

> Remember, an angel with a flaming rod
> Drove Man from Paradise.

> He set a gulf before the gate.
> Over that gulf you cannot leap.
>
> (P. 153)

The fjord, which the townspeople dare not cross to save the murderer's soul, is another such gulf. Ibsen sees the human soul, not as continuously progressing and improving, but rather as developing in great leaps, each involving a courageous choice. The influence of Kierkegaard is strong here, and, as I shall soon attempt to show, that influence pervades the rest of the play as well. Ibsen takes Kierkegaard's concept of the leap of the soul, the individual's sudden self-transformation, and embodies it in literal movement across some gap, as in the trip across the water, or in verbal metaphors such as the one about the angel's setting a gulf before the gate of paradise.

Agnes and Brand travel safely across the fjord, and the terror-stricken murderer dies peacefully. Act 3 takes place three years later. Brand has become the town priest, and has married Agnes. On this particular day, Brand's mother, a materialistic character like the rest of the villagers, lies dying. She asks for her son to come to her; he refuses to go unless she repents. She offers to give up half her treasure. Since this is the worst possible response for Brand, whose motto is "All or Nothing," he allows her to die alone. Again Ibsen uses physical separation to symbolize a separation of souls. Brand cannot go to his mother until she reaches his level of ethical commitment. This generates an ambivalent attitude in the audience toward him, since he seems so callous, but since Ibsen sees man in terms of absolutes, and is writing a play about the necessity for choice, this ambivalence is inevitable. If the choices were easy, the play would be trivial. The audience's ambivalent feelings are shared by some of the characters in the play itself, such as Brand's mother's doctor, who is *not* one of the hypocritical characters:[3]

> Our generation is not to be scared by rods
> Of fire, or by nurses' tales about damned souls.
> Its first commandment, Brand, is: Be humane.
>
> (P. 101)

But Brand replies scornfully, "Humane! That word excuses all our weakness."

Brand and Agnes have a child, who is unhealthy because of the severe climate, in the small valley where

> There's no light or sunshine. . . .
> The wind cuts like a polar blast;
> The clammy mist never lifts.
>
> (P. 102)

Another winter would kill the boy. Brand agrees to travel south, to save his son's life, but the Doctor reminds him that he would be fleeing from his calling as a preacher. Brand stays and the child dies. Critics have faulted this whole incident as extremely contrived: in the first place, a trip to a mild climate is no guarantee of recovery for a tubercular patient (a fact that Ibsen, with his interest in medicine, ought to have known), and in the second place, why does Brand not merely send his family south without him? As is often the case, Ibsen is more concerned with establishing an extreme situation, a crucial choice, than with getting all the details right. But there is an additional sidelight. Ibsen wrote the play shortly after arriving in Italy, having just left Norway for the first time in his life. The trip made a powerful impression on him, especially his first sight of Italy:

> Over the high mountains the clouds hung like great, dark curtains, and beneath these we drove through the tunnel and, suddenly, found ourselves at Mira Mara, where that marvelously bright light which is the beauty of the south suddenly revealed itself to me, gleaming like white marble. It was to affect all my later work.[4]

The imagery of mountains and mist, and the sun breaking through, is almost identical to that of *Brand*. This experience was indeed to affect all of Ibsen's later work. From then on, the South in his plays is generally associated with light, pleasure, vitality, and (as in *Brand*) health, while the North is associated with darkness or mistiness, duty, narrowness, and illness. In other words, Ibsen was not really a realist by temperament; he was more interested in transforming his emotional reaction to the South into symbols and metaphors in his plays than he was in the scientific causes and cures of disease. His fascination with the symbolic possibilities of locale, at the expense of scientific accuracy, is a cause for many of the complaints that are leveled at his drama. We shall reencounter this particular symbol, of the South as magic cure-all, in *A Doll House*, where it has also been grounds for much critical caviling.

The opposing duality of mist and light pervades all of *Brand*. The stage directions for the opening scene state, "*Mist hangs densely. It is raining, and nearly dark*" (p. 51). Brand himself is a dark figure, "*dressed in black*" (p. 51), who speaks "*from the mist*" (p. 54). Yet when Ejnar and Agnes appear in this first scene (Agnes of course not yet being converted), the mist clears:

> *Ejnar and Agnes, warm and glowing, in light traveling clothes, come dancing along the edge of the crevasse. The mist has dispersed, and a clear summer morning lies over the mountain.*
>
> (P. 55)

Thus the rationale for allowing the child to die, in Act 3, is clear in a symbolic sense. Both Brand and Agnes must remain in Norway, in the dark, cold valley where "the clammy mist never lefts" because they are "misty" characters. After Agnes has converted, she becomes a dark, dutiful person like her husband; for her to travel south with her child, so sensible in a logical, naturalistic sense, would be metaphorically inappropriate for her character-type as Ibsen has created it at that moment. The logical "mistake" is the result of poetic necessity.

In Act 4 the confrontation is between Brand and Agnes. Agnes has clung to the memory of her child, and has saved his clothes almost like religious relics. A gypsy appears, who needs the clothing for her own suffering child. Brand insists that Agnes give the clothing up; she does so only after a severe inner struggle, which ends in her own death. Her decision is another great character transformation, similar to her earlier one by the fjord. This time she achieves a strange serenity, which leaves her husband baffled:

> AGNES. Yes, I have conquered now. Conquered death.
> And fear. He was born to die. Ulf is in heaven.
> If I dared, if I could, I would not beg for him back
>   again.
> Giving my child has saved my soul from death.
> Thank you for guiding my hand. You have fought for
>   me
> Unflinchingly. Now the weight has fallen on you—
> Of All or Nothing. Now you stand
> In the valley of choice.
> BRAND. Agnes, you speak in riddles. Our struggle is
>   over.
> AGNES. Have you forgotten, Brand?
> He dies who sees Jehovah face to face.
> BRAND. No! Agnes, no! You shall not leave me.
> Let me lose everything else, everything,
> But not you. Don't leave me, Agnes!
>
> (Pp. 125-26)

As with the trip south, no scientific explanation is given for Agnes's death. Her death is used instead as a metaphor for a change in a state of being. Once again a great gulf has opened between the two characters; at the beginning of the play, Agnes was beneath Brand spiritually, but now she is above him, in a state that is beyond his reach or understanding.

Act 5 begins with a new setting, in front of the new church that Brand had challenged the villagers to build. The Mayor and Provost of the town are of course delighted with the fine new church, but only in the spirit of Chamber of Commerce boosterism; Brand finds himself dissatisfied. The strange mountain girl, Gerd, had mentioned earlier a church of ice, high in the mountains. Brand leads the villagers up to it. At first they follow eagerly, but gradually fall away, lured back down by a lie of the Mayor's about a huge school of fish that has just entered the fjord that will bring prosperity to the town. Alone, Brand again meets Gerd, who sees in him the reincarnation of Christ, in the passage already quoted:

> GERD. You're the Big Man. The Biggest of all.
> BRAND. I used to think I was.
> GERD. Let me see your hands.
> BRAND. My hands?
> GERD. They're scarred with nails. There's blood in your hair.
> The thorn's teeth have cut your forehead.
> You've been on the cross. My father told me
> It happened long ago and far away.
> But now I see he was deceiving me.
> I know you. You are the Saviour Man!
> (Pp. 154-55)

But, especially since the death of his wife, Brand has realized the weakness in his own character; the final scene can be viewed as Brand's confrontation with himself, and finally with God. When Gerd calls Brand "The Greatest of all," Brand can only reply, "I am the meanest thing that crawls on earth" (p. 155).

A huge white hawk, which had appeared earlier in the

scene, as well as in Act 1, suddenly reappears in the sky. Gerd shoots it with her rifle, and as the hawk falls it turns into an avalanche that fills the whole valley and buries them both. As it rushes down, Brand shouts, "Answer me, God, in the moment of death!/If not by Will, how can Man be redeemed?" (p. 157). The final sound is a voice, through the thundering avalanche, which cries, "He is the God of Love," implying that Brand was wrong in his austere, willful approach to life—and yet, what kind of "Love" is this, that kills not only Gerd and Brand, but destroyed Agnes as well? If the Will is ultimately evil, yet "He dies who sees Jehovah face to face," what alternative exists? With this bleak, enigmatic conclusion, *Brand* is surely one of the most pessimistic tragedies ever written.

It is impossible to do justice to this turbulent, complex, and evocative play in the brief description above. The play is vastly underrecognized, and should not only be read as an introduction to Ibsen's realistic plays, but read and produced as a great tragedy in its own right. Yet, for all its complexity, a good deal of *Brand's* structure becomes clear if the play is viewed through the philosophy of Søren Kierkegaard. Unfortunately, this is the very play for which Ibsen specifically denied a Kierkegaardian influence, in the letter already quoted:

> It is a great mistake to suppose that I have depicted the life and career of Kierkegaard (I have read very little of Kierkegaard and understood even less). That Brand is a clergyman is really immaterial.[5]

A close reading of this passage, however, reveals that Ibsen was speaking of only a single aspect of the play—the characterization of Brand himself—and denying that it was based on the actual life and career of Kierkegaard. He was not talking about the play as a whole, its themes or its structure. Whether Brand the character is based on Kierkegaard the person is actually irrelevant; it is not so much the personality of Kierkegaard that is important to understanding *Brand* as it is Kierkegaard's philosophy, which provides the structural underpinning for the play. Indeed, Kierkegaardian philosophy provides an almost indispensable map for understanding all of Ibsen's plays, including the later, realistic ones.

It is difficult to reduce Kierkegaard's theories to simple formulae, since he generally wrote obscurely, in a first-person, quasi-novel form, under various pseudonyms. But since my purpose is not to provide a guide to Kierkegaard but rather to Ibsen, I shall attempt it, with apologies to Kierkegaard scholars. Specifically, Kierkegaard's philosophy is a reaction to the philosophy of Hegel, whose ideas Kierkegaard felt tended to reduce the individual to a mere part of a grandiose historical system, but more generally it is a reaction to the scientific spirit that dominated the middle of the nineteenth century. This spirit, which tends to see life in objective, positivistic, evolutionary terms, can be seen expressed in the philosophy of Hegel (and later, of Marx), the sociological theories of men like Comte and Taine, the biological theories of Darwin, and ultimately the realistic movement in literature. All of these were optimistic in their own terms, in that they saw life as gradually becoming better, but at the same time they all posited a system in which individual life tended to become secondary.

Some men, though living out their private lives in quiet desperation, are able to find consolation in the fact that their nation is becoming stronger, their race advancing, their "class" triumphing over reaction. Not Kierkegaard. For him the basic reality was not found in these grandiose schemes, but rather in the validity of the individual life. He saw life as progressing through distinct stages of personal development, analogous to the way society passes through stages of historical development according to the philosophy of Hegel, except that the process for Kierkegaard was not social but rather a matter of individual free will. In other words, Kierkegaard saw man in fundamentally Romantic terms, not dominated by his environment, but rather capable of choosing among ideal lifestyles.

Kierkegaard identified three distinct stages of individual existence: the aesthetic, the ethical, and the religious. The first two are described extensively in his two-volume work *Either/Or,* written in 1843, and the third in his book *Fear and Trembling,* completed in the same year. Although each stage is higher and better than the previous, each has its own purpose and validity. The aesthetic man lives for self-gratification; the ethical for duty; the religious for faith. Even though something like self-gratification may seem ignoble, a person whose dedication to it is total has a validity that makes him in a way as worthy as those who are totally dedicated to duty or faith; for Kierkegaard, validity means having total self-commitment to a single passion, as opposed to having divided commitments.

The aesthetic man, living for pleasure, is utterly amoral. "*Summa summarum:* I do not care at all,"[6] writes Kierkegaard in his aesthetic persona. The aesthetic man's philosophy, if it can be called that, is *carpe diem,* seize the day, live for the moment. "Time flows, life is a stream, people say, and so on. I do not notice it. Time stands still, and I with it."[7] Life is a continuing series of new sensations and new gratifications, always new and yet somehow always the same. Everything changes, yet nothing changes. The aesthetic man is a man of the masses, "only one thread among many, which must be woven into the fabric of life!"[8] Yet a prime example of this type is the artist, in the nineteenth-century sense of the bohemian lover of pleasure and beauty; hence the term *aesthetic.*

The ethical man, by contrast, lives for duty and personal

vocation. Duty for him is not merely an externally imposed obligation, an onerous necessity, but part of his very being, an inner compulsion: "He has clad himself in duty, for him it is the expression of his inmost nature."[9] He is often a leader, and relates to others as a society, with patterns of relationships and codes of behavior (which he may try to make people live up to, or to change) rather than as "masses." He loves "the univeral," in the Kantian sense, where each human action must be weighed as though it were a universal principle. As Ibsen's Brand says, "I know but one law for all mankind. / I cannot discriminate" (p. 96). There are no exceptions, no special cases, not even, as in Brand's case, for one's own mother. A prime example of this type is found in the Bible, in the character of Job, who remains passionately devoted to a moral code despite terrible suffering, challenging the beliefs of his friends and even demanding an explanation from God himself.

The religious man, the highest of all, is a person of infinite resignation. Not even the universal tempts him; living for faith, he can commit acts that seem immoral or absurd. He can relate to others as individuals, rather than as "society," and make special cases because faith can transcend the rational. (In this, he strangely resembles the aesthetic man.) A prime example of this type, which Kierkegaard deals with extensively in *Fear and Trembling*, is Abraham in the biblical story of Abraham and Isaac. Abraham's willingness to obey God's command to sacrifice his son Isaac, proved by Abraham's actual raising of the knife, is clearly an absurd, religious act. He cannot be considered an aesthetic man, since he experiences no pleasure in killing his son—he naturally loathes the very thought of it. Yet he cannot be considered ethical, since killing one's son is absurd from that point of view as well. Applying Kant's categorical imperative, by "universalizing" the sacrifice of one's children, one ultimately puts an end to the human race, and thus has no more children to sacrifice! Abraham's act is thus one of infinite resignation to God's will, a special case that is completely unethical yet in fact religious.

It should be stressed that these stages are to be considered totally separate, and that to move upward from one to another is a matter of a great leap, rather than of gradual development. A novel like *War and Peace,* in which Pierre slowly and with much backsliding develops into an ethical person, presents a view of life that is *not* Kierkegaardian. For Kierkegaard, transformations are sudden, total, and traumatic. Job did not achieve the religious stage of life in a continuous development from the ethical stage. In fact, he was so committed to ethics that he was prepared to call God into account for the lack of justice in the world. He would have remained in the ethical stage forever, if God had not challenged him, demonstrating the paltriness of Job's human viewpoint. Then Job *renounced* the ethical stage and leaped to the religious.

Nevertheless, the fact that gradual development is not possible does not mean that intermediates do not exist. But these intermediates are not stages in the same sense that the aesthetic, ethical, and religious are, because they lack validity. They are a kind of shadowy, half existence, worse even than the stage immediately below. Kierkegaard described the state between aesthetic and ethical as "ironic"; a person in such a state is a hypocrite, moral in theory and self-seeking in practice. (The distinction between a conscious and an unconscious hypocrite, which interested Ibsen as it did Stendhal, does not seem to have concerned Kierkegaard.) The state between ethical and religious Kierkegaard called "humorous," a word that seems strange in its application until one recognizes that, as with the ironic level, there is a ludicrous contrast when a supposed devotion to a higher level is associated with an actual devotion to a lower. When Ann Landers promotes religion on the grounds that "the family that prays together, stays together," she is reducing religion to a mere adjunct, a means to an end that might well be accomplished differently. Plenty of families stay together without religion; many religious families have broken apart. (Certainly Abraham's was about to!) The intermediate "ironic" and "humorous" levels, then, are a counterfeit form of existence. In making the leap between aesthetic and ethical, or ethical and religious, the validly developing individual will bypass them.

The Kierkegaardian triad of character types, with the intermediate levels, and the concept of the leap from one level to another, inform all of Ibsen's work from *Brand* onwards. This is not to say that Ibsen was merely a pamphleteer for Kierkegaard, any more than he was a pamphleteer for feminism or water purification. Ibsen's treatment of the various levels is often different from Kierkegaard's, even varying from play to play. In *Brand*, for example, the religious level seems to be equated with death—"He dies who sees Jehovah face to face"—something not found in Kierkegaard himself, who was, when all was said and done, a fairly optimistic philosopher. There were other influences on Ibsen than that of Kierkegaard: as Brian Johnston has exhaustively shown, Ibsen's sense of historical development seems to come from Hegel. The pessimism in *Brand* and some of the later plays can be traced to Schopenhauer, with his theory of the Will as inevitably evil, even when bent on doing good. Brand is an ethical man in the Kierkegaardian sense, but has the additional quality of believing in, and being driven by, the Will, to which he makes frequent appeals throughout the play:

> It is not by spectacular achievements
> That man can be transformed, but by will.
> It is man's will that acquits or condemns him.
>
> (P. 86)

Brand's final line in the play, in which he begs God to tell him "If not by Will, how can Man be redeemed?" which is answered by his own destruction in the avalanche and the voice crying "He is the God of Love," is almost pure Schopenhauer. Finally, as with any writer, there are personal elements in Ibsen's work in addition to "influences." As James Kerans has pointed out in an admirable essay,[10] the motif of *Kindermord,* or child-killing, is strongly present in every Ibsen play from *Brand* onwards. In *Brand,* of course, it appears in the death of Brand's child, Ulf, and the child-murderer whom Brand and Agnes go to save in Act 2. Ulf's death can be seen in Schopenhauerian terms, with Brand's Will, though aimed at doing good, destroying a beloved child; it can also be seen in terms of the Abraham and Isaac story dealt with in *Fear and Trembling.* But the underlying, driving force behind these *Kindermord* incidents is undoubtedly Ibsen's shame at having fathered an illegitimate child, which haunted him all his life.

Thus, Kierkegaard should never be regarded as the be-all and end-all with Ibsen; Kierkegaard's philosophy will be shown to be in the substructure of the plays rather than the superstructure, the bones rather than the flesh. It is analogous to the "Chain of Being" concept, which has been applied so fruitfully to Shakespeare, operating at an unconscious, almost automatic level, which is rarely made explicit in the plays yet operates in every one of them. The Kierkegaardian triad is necessary to the understanding of Ibsen, but never sufficient in itself to explain him.

In *Brand,* every character can be seen in Kierkegaardian terms. Brand himself is an ethical character striving for the religious, while Agnes is a character who progresses through all three levels. In the first act, when she is dancing through the mountains with Ejnar, she is aesthetic; she leaps to the ethical when she gets into the boat with Brand; after the death of her child, in the gypsy scene where she attempts to cling to the child's memory, she is "humorous" (an unfortunate term to apply to such a grim state, yet it perhaps helps to describe her disequilibrium at that point in the play); and she becomes religious when she gives up that last scrap of the child's clothing, and dies.

With the final transformation of Agnes, Brand finds himself in the humorous state, "in the valley of choice" (p. 126) as Agnes puts it. His moral commitment, which led to the deaths of Ulf and Agnes, turns out to have been a temptation, driven by pride rather than genuine love of God. In the final act, Brand has a confrontation that drives home his own inadequacy: Ejnar, Agnes's former fiancé, the painter who had been so typically and happily aesthetic in Act 1, reappears. He too has undergone a drastic transformation, brought about by a severe illness:

> I became a preacher of total abstinence,
> And am now a missionary.
>
> (P. 138)

But his new ethical state is so extreme as to make him into a ghastly parody of Brand himself. Ejnar cannot even remember Agnes's name (like Brand, he "knows but one law for all Mankind"), is only concerned with how she died, and denounces everything earthly, including human love, as "vanity, vanity" (p. 139). Concerning the ultimate inadequacy of the ethical man, Kierkegaard had written:

> Whoever has had inwardness enough to lay hold of the ethical with infinite passion, and to understand the eternal validity of duty and the universal, for him there can neither in heaven or on earth or in hell be found so

fearful a plight, as when he faces a collision *where the ethical becomes a temptation*.[11] [My italics]

Now, at the end of the play, the ethical tempts man to arrogance, as it had often done with Brand. In this confrontation with Ejnar, this awful mirror of himself, Brand's personal ambiguity becomes clear. While Brand was genuinely heroic, and certainly superior to, say, the villagers, his tendencies toward self-dramatization and fanaticism are decided flaws. He has always told *others* what to do, but has rarely looked inward. Until the final act, *he* had made no sacrifices, but had only demanded them of others; now he must sacrifice his own pride, and see himself as "the meanest thing that crawls on earth." Only thus can he reach the religious level, but, as with Agnes, reaching it means death.

It is now possible to chart the various characters in *Brand* according to a Kierkegaardian scheme:

AESTHETIC	*Ironic*	ETHICAL	*Humorous*	RELIGIOUS
Ejnar (Acts 1 & 2)	Villagers	Brand (Acts 1 –4)	Brand (Act 5)	Brand (end)
Agnes (Act 1)	Mayor	Agnes (Acts 2 –3)	Agnes (Act 4)	Agnes (end of Act 4)
Provost	Child-Murderer	Ejnar (Act 5)		
Ulf	Brand's Mother	Doctor		
	Sexton, Guide, Schoolmaster, etc.			

I shall not deal with the lesser characters in detail, nor distinguish between the conscious and unconscious hypocrites at the ironic level, as I shall in treating the social plays. The chart does enable us to see how Ibsen's drama works in terms of characterization and plot; the characters are created as types, rather than developing from psychological "motivations," and the plot moves in leaps, as the characters change, rather than unfolding gradually.

The Kierkegaardian pattern of stages operates not only on characterization and plot in *Brand,* but upon symbolism as well. There are, for example, three churches in the play, the villagers' old church, "little" and "ugly" (p. 115); the new church that the villagers build at Brand's urging; and an "ice church" high in the mountains:

> BRAND. When I was a boy, up among the peaks and summits,
> At the head of a valley, there was a chasm.
> People called it the Ice Church.
> A frozen mountain lake was its floor.
> And a great piled snowdrift stretched like a roof
> Over the split in the mountain wall.
> (P. 66)

The three churches represent the ironic, ethical, and religious levels; it is immediately after the confrontation with Ejnar, in Act 5, that Brand sees the inadequacy of the church that has just been built, and leads the villagers up the mountain in search of "The Church of Life" (p. 142). And it is the "great piled snowdrift" that forms the avalanche that engulfs Brand at the end.

Crevasses and the fjord in the play generally stand for the gaps between the three levels; but there is also a triad of mountain, town, and sea that seem to reflect the religious, ethical, and aesthetic levels respectively. North and South seem to stand for the ethical and the aesthetic (a polarity that is developed in *Peer Gynt* and later plays). Light, dark, and mist are important in the play, but here the symbolism is a bit more complex. Darkness, mist, and blackness (both Brand and Ejnar after his transformation are described as dressed in black) are generally associated with the ethical level; but light and warmth appear to be associated with both the aesthetic *and* the religious. The sun breaks through the mist and shines on the dancing Agnes and Ejnar in Act 1, and candlelight is an important symbol associated with the child, Ulf:

> Last Christmas he groped
> With his tiny fingers at their clear flames.
> He stretched forward from his little chair and asked:
> "Mother, is it the sun?"
>
> (P. 119)

But light also seems to be associated with the religious level, as when toward the end of the play Brand again and again calls for "Light, light!" as an expression of his inner longing for something more meaningful than his ethical existence. Agnes announces her religious transfiguration metaphorically as a sunrise:

> The darkness is past. The mist is stolen away.
> The clouds have gone. Through the night, beyond death,
> I see the morning.
>
> (P. 125)

Similarly, the clouds lift to expose the ice church just before Brand's death. All this symbolism, much of which recurs in Ibsen's later plays, can be charted as follows:

AESTHETIC	ETHICAL	RELIGIOUS
Old Church	New Church	Ice Church
light, color	mist, darkness, blackness	light, clarity
sea	town	mountain
South	North	
warmth	coldness	
Artist	Preacher	

The ambiguity of light as warmth and vitality versus light as blazing clarity or truth is particularly Ibsenish. Note that not all the symbol sets, reading horizontally, have an equivalent in the "religious" column, reflecting the remote and problematic nature of that level, which is the least completely realized in the play. In many of his other plays, particularly those of his middle period, Ibsen was not much concerned with that level at all, but dealt exclusively with problems arising from the conflict between the aesthetic and the ethical. This is what makes them seem to be peculiarly "social problem plays," although in every case the specific social problem is subordinated to the *personal* problem of individual development.

Behind the problems of the individual development of his characters lay Ibsen's own personal problems. His whole adult life can be viewed as being torn between an aesthetic orientation and a desire to seem ethical; he was, alas, a perfect example of Kierkegaard's "ironic" man. On the one hand he was Ibsen the social critic; on the other, Ibsen the artist. His ethical side is seen in his bourgeois life style, his devotion to his wife and son, his regular working habits, his delight in medals and honors, and his terror of scandal. Halvdan Koht, Ibsen's first major biographer, relates an anecdote that sums up this side of Ibsen: In his impoverished youth, he would often put on his one and only suit of good clothes, leave his rooming house as if headed for a restaurant, and then sneak back to his room for a simple meal of bread and cheese.[12] Even in his early years, he was painfully in need of maintaining a fine reputation; later in life, having won world renown through his plays, Ibsen returned to Norway, where he would sit for hours in an Oslo cafe, dressed to the hilt, wearing all his medals. Yet, the other side of Ibsen can be seen in his fathering an illegitimate child, his drinking bouts, his love of Italy and the South, and his affairs with young girls. As for *Brand,* it was of course the play that first made his reputation, establishing Ibsen as a stern moralist, but the story of its original publication sheds light on the two-sided Ibsen. Ibsen mailed the manuscript from Italy to his Norwegian publisher, surprisingly named Hegel.[13] Hegel wanted Ibsen (who had been known as an ardent Norwegian nationalist) to change the Norwegian orthography of the play so that more Danes would buy the book. Ibsen agreed. Hegel also insisted on printing only half an edition (625 copies), with half the usual royalty, because he was afraid that the public would not like a long, poetic drama. Ibsen meekly agreed to that as well.[14] All or Nothing?

Peer Gynt, written immediately after *Brand,* is a depiction of the aesthetic man; the two plays taken together can be seen as Ibsen's *Either/Or.*[15] It is interesting to study the two plays together, since not only the two title characters, but also many of the incidents, and the dominant symbolism of each, are such clear contrasts. *Peer Gynt,* like *Brand,* is constructed as a series of confrontations; but where Brand welcomes and even intensifies each new challenge, Peer meets each one with evasion. Where Brand's motto was "All or Nothing," Peer's is supplied for him by the Great Boyg, an invisible monster whom he confronts in Act 2: "Go roundabout" (pp. 94-95).

The sphere of action in *Brand* is exceedingly limited, to one small Norwegian town and its environs. *Peer Gynt* is wide ranging, as Peer travels all over the world, to America, China, Europe, Africa, and finally home to Norway. Similarly, *Brand* takes place over a relatively short time—a few years at most—while *Peer Gynt* covers almost an entire lifetime, from the time Peer leaves Norway as a youth until his return as a grizzled old man. *Brand,* as we saw, was a play dominated by coldness, mist, darkness, gloom; *Peer Gynt,* on the other hand, is a play of warmth, sunlight, color, laughter—the perfect answer to those who accuse the Norwegian playwright of being humorless and morbid. Both plays may be ultimately tragic, but *Peer Gynt* is filled with delightful poetry, hilarious satire, and mischievous surprises. When Peer, shipwrecked and drowning, is reassured by a passenger swimming casually past that "No one dies half through the last act" (p. 197), we know we are in a world far different from the austere, unrelenting *Brand.*

Peer Gynt, like so many nineteenth-century plays, is based on Goethe's *Faust,* except that Peer is not a scholar but *l'homme moyen sensuel.* Peer leaves his native Norway to travel around the world, always awaited at home by his faithful girl friend Solveig, who is devoted to Peer as Margaret was to Faust. In his travels, Peer encounters trolls and other supernatural creatures, mysterious strangers, and (especially) girls; after many adventures, he returns as an old man to Norway and Solveig, who is strangely unchanged. In a scene that foreshadows the ending of *Ghosts,* the play ends as the sun rises, with Peer sleeping in Solveig's arms. She is a kind of eternal mother figure, and Peer has reverted to the role of a child; in the early morning light, she sings:

> Sleep in my arms; I'll watch over thee—
> Sleep and dream, my dearest boy!
>
> (P. 240)

The character of Peer is based on a folk figure, who may actually have existed, that Ibsen learned about in travels through rural Norway. Peer is lazy, greedy (in an insouciant sort of way), sexually amoral, and a fantastic liar. In the very first scene, we see him telling a long, elaborate, yet fascinating lie to his mother, Aase, about capturing a reindeer, riding on its back, leaping over a steep cliff, crashing with it into a lake below, and escaping unharmed. He tells the story so well that his mother is overwhelmed with excitement, yet suddenly she remembers that she has heard it all before:

> Oh, you tricky little devil—
> God in heaven, you can lie!
> I remember all this drivel
> Now; it happened to Gudbrand
> Glesne, back when I was twenty.
> This is his ride secondhand,
> Not your own, you—!
>
> (P. 35)

After a bit of raillery, Peer lifts his mother to his back, crying, "I'm the reindeer, you be Peer!" (p. 43), and ends the scene by lifting her to the top of the millhouse roof, where she remains stranded. A motif is established here that operates ceaselessly throughout the play: While Brand *led* people, Peer "carries" them, both literally and figuratively. That is, he literally abducts them, like the bride in the following scene, and several more girls in succeeding scenes; and he also "carries them away" in a figurative sense, with his lies and play-acting. A poignant example occurs in Act 3, when in the midst of his travels Peer returns briefly to visit his mother, who is dying. In typical fashion, he comforts her with a little play, pretending to be driving her to heaven, with her bed a fine sleigh, and himself the driver, peremptorily demanding entrance for her from Saint Peter. She dies happily; he closes her eyes and bends over her:

> Here's thanks for all of your days,
> For the blows and the kisses I had—
> But give back some little praise—
> *(Presses his cheek to her mouth.)*
> There—that was thanks for the ride.
>
> (P. 120)

This scene shows that it is quite possible for the aesthetic man to feel tenderness, love, and devotion. It is not the austere, demanding love of a Brand, of course, but simple, human, spontaneous warmth—poignant yet temporary, for the moment his mother is dead, Peer is off on his travels again, with never another thought of her. Yet this scene contrasts with the crucial scene in *Brand*, when, as a result of his style of love, Brand does not return to *his* dying mother, who dies alone and uncomforted.

It is important to the understanding of the plays to see that both Peer and Brand are right in what they do. Ibsen was like a modern existentialist; morals for him were a matter of circumstance and one's level of personal commitment, rather than abstract rules. In Kierkegaard's actual words, one is "either a parson/or an actor";[16] the parson must refuse to go to his mother, while the actor must not.

As in *Brand*, in *Peer Gynt* the various secondary characters mirror the title character, either directly or by contrast. The trolls, quite frightening at first, turn out to be much like Peer. Their motto, explains the Troll King, is "Troll, to yourself be—enough!" (p. 85). This of course suits Peer just fine—it has in effect been his own motto all along—and he is all set to become a troll himself until he learns that it involves an irreversible eye operation. The only difference between trolls and men, it appears, is that trolls are incapable of change, while human beings are capable of the leap to the ethical. Since Peer wants to keep the option of changing (although of course he never actually does), he refuses the operation, and barely escapes from the trolls with his life.

A contrasting character, whom Peer sees but never meets, is a young boy who cuts off a finger to avoid the draft (a moral problem as prevalent in the nineteenth century as in our supposedly more enlightened one). Once again it is an irreversible "operation," this time involving commitment to the ethical level. Peer finds it interesting, but is unable to conceive actually *doing* it:

> They want to send him to war;
> And the boy, of course, doesn't want to go—
> But to cut off—? For all time, never to—
> Yes, think it; wish it; *will* it so—
> But to *do* it! No, that's not for Peer.
>
> (P. 102)

This boy commits himself for all time, but for Peer it is merely another interesting observation, something to think about. He can never do such a thing, but can only seek new experiences, new sensations, new ideas that do not change *him*, and hence are in effect no change at all. Years later, when Peer returns to Norway as an old man, he hears a sermon preached in which the life of this contemporary of his is described. The boy was steadfast to his principles, withstood the ostracism of the town, built a house for himself "high in the mountains" (p. 199), fought the elements, raised a family (who showed him no gratitude), and finally died, alone and unappreciated. Yet despite this, his life had dignity and purpose; "he was great, because he was himself" (p. 200), says the preacher. A dichotomy is set up in the play between one's moral self, to which one must be true ("Man, to yourself be true!" is the ideal among men, according to the Troll King), and one's carnal self, or "Gyntian self," to which one must be merely "enough":

> The Gyntian self—it's an army corps
> Of wishes, appetites, desires.
> The Gyntian self is a churning sea
> Of whims, demands, necessities.
>
> (P. 132)

In Kierkegaardian terms, the moral self is the ethical, and the "Gyntian self" the aesthetic. An important point the play makes is that the ethical is not merely ordinary, Christmas-card morality. The boy who cut off his finger was immoral from society's point of view; the ethical is an *inner* state, and one is ethical when one is true to one's *own* morality. (We hardly notice that Peer has also avoided the draft, simply by not being around when it was called; this is an aesthetic response to the same problem as the boy's.) The preacher says of the boy:

> Lost to his country's laws? Yes, if you want.
> But one true light above the law prevails.
>
> (P. 200)

Just as the Mayor in *Brand* could mouth pious platitudes without being truly ethical, so the boy can be genuinely so despite society's bad concept of him. This is of course a theme that Ibsen is famous for, which is important in all the social plays.

Another strikingly ethical character in the play is Solveig, whose unchanging steadfastness (she apparently does not even grow old) contrasts sharply with Peer's incessant affairs with the women he meets on his journeys: mountain girls, the daughter of the Troll King, the daughter of a Bedouin chief, and so on. Solveig, like Brand, lives out her life in a small hut in a snowy valley near an obscure Norwegian town. She too is true to her ideal, which for her (surprisingly enough) is Peer. Morality is again a question of attitude; the girls love Peer, and he them, in an aesthetic way, while Solveig loves Peer in a dedicated, idealized, ethical way.

It is now possible to place the characters on a scale, somewhat reminiscent of the one for *Brand:*

AESTHETIC	ETHICAL
Peer Gynt	Boy with 4 fingers
Troll King	Preacher
Mountain Girls	
Troll King's daughter	
Anitra	Solveig
Villagers	Aase (Peer's mother)
Trolls	
Weird creatures (Boyg, Sphinx, Statue of Memnon, Button Moulder)	
Other adventurers	
Animals	

It is of course fitting that the right-hand column be considerably shorter than the left, since the ethical person is rare even in life. In the play, none of them is on stage for very long; they serve more as counterpoints than as fullfledged characters in a work that is, after all, a study of the aesthetic type. But note also that Ibsen is not much concerned here with the in-between, ironic level, which was so important in *Brand,* and the religious level is not in evidence either. On the other hand, the theme of *repetition* is much more prevalent; characters reflect not only Peer but each other. An important development, as the play progresses, is that everyone starts to look the same. (Many would of course be played by the same actors, since the enormous cast of characters requires much doubling and tripling of roles.) In the Egyptian desert, Peer notices that the statue of Memnon looks like the King of the Trolls, while the Sphinx reminds him of the Great Boyg (p. 166). Anitra, the Bedouin chief's daughter, acts very much like the Troll King's daughter. The monkeys in Act 4 behave like the trolls in Act 2; Peer even uses the same line to refer to both: "The old one's foul, but the children are worse!" (pp. 93, 142).

References to animals abound in the play; animals mentioned include a pig, horse, monkeys, reindeer, goat, cows, eagles, birds, herring, hornet, fish, camel, cat, dog, lion, elephant, lizards, and owl. Peer himself rides on reindeer (at least in his imagination), a white horse, and a pig; he is compared to a beast, a goat, and a pig when he carries off the bride in Act 1 (p. 67); and he is described elsewhere as a "beast" (p. 101). The obvious point is that the aesthetic life is like that of an animal, driven by instinct and appetite alone, without a "true self" or soul. This point is reinforced in the famous onion scene, in which Peer peels layer after layer from an onion, looking for its kernel, only to find that, like himself, it has none:

> This outer layer, like a torn coat—
> It's the shipwrecked man on the drifting boat.
> Here's the passenger layer, thin as paint—
> But the taste has a dash of the real Peer Gynt.
> The prospector life was a run for the money;
> The juice is gone—if it ever had any.
> And now this rough-skinned layer—why,
> That's the fur trader up at Hudson's Bay.
> The next resembles a crown—no, thanks!
> That we'll throw away—it's a jinx.
> Here's the archaeologist, brief and brassy.
> And here's the prophet, green and juicy.
> He stinks, as the Scripture says, of lies,
> Enough to bring tears to an honest man's eyes.
> This layer that curls in softly together
> Is the man of the world, living for pleasure.
> The next looks sick. It has streaks of black—
> Meaning priests—and slaves on the auction block.
>   *(Pulls off several layers at once.)*
> These layers just go endlessly on!
> Shouldn't it give up its kernel soon?
>   *(Pulls the whole onion apart.)*
> God, but it doesn't! To the innermost filler,
> It's nothing but layers—smaller and smaller—
> Nature is witty!
>   (Pp. 208-9)

The great theme of the play is that a life of continual change turns out to be merely a life of continual repetition. The layers of the onion at first appear to be all fascinatingly different, but they "go endlessly on" until all look alike, except smaller and smaller. Peer's lust for experience leads him to an endless variety of sensations that are, at bottom, all the same, except more and more trivial. Even his death, it appears, will lead to more repetition; in one of those zany oddities that the play is full of, a "Button Moulder" appears on the scene in Act 5, complete with casting ladle, to inform Peer that since he has no self, he is to be melted down in a pot with all of his kind, from which others will be recast. But even *that* does not take place in any decisive way; the Button Moulder just keeps warning Peer over and over that it will happen "at the next crossroads," and the play ends with Peer in Solveig's arms. The "recasting," one might say, has occurred symbolically, with Peer reverting to his childhood; but even *then*, the Button Moulder continues to warn about "the final crossroads" (p. 240) as the curtain falls.

There is a strange similarity between the ethical and the aesthetic types, apparent as we see the two leading examples, Solveig and Peer, embracing at the end: Solveig has remained faithful to her true self, unchanging even to the point of not aging. Yet she appears to have been transformed into Peer's mother, or rather into a kind of universal mother, the very ideal of motherhood. Peer has lived through incessant changes, yet at the end is unchanged, or rather, back to where he started. Neither has developed a true, unique self. Since the play does not deal with the religious type, this ambiguity remains unresolved. The problem with the ethical is that the person becomes identified with the ideal, the universal, thus turning into an abstract type. The problem with the aesthetic is that one is continually dying—"to be yourself is to slay yourself" (p.

227), says the Button Moulder—yet continually being reborn; it is like the oriental view of existence as an endless cycle of death and reincarnation from which man must try to escape.

In *The Quintessence of Ibsenism,* Bernard Shaw remarks facetiously that "whether or no it was better to be Peer Gynt than Brand, it was beyond all question better to be the mother or the sweetheart of Peer, scapegrace and liar as he was, than mother or wife to the saintly Brand."[17] But it is a question of one's point of view. Since Brand leads people, rather than "carrying" them, he appeals to the best in them, rather than playing on their weaknesses. English-speaking people have traditionally been suspicious of idealists; we tend to prefer Falstaff to Hotspur, Sancho Panza to Don Quixote, and thus Peer Gynt to Brand. But while we may find Peer Gynt's insouciance charming, and Brand's moral intensity insufferable, we cannot automatically say that one is better than the other. The plays make it clear that both characters are morally ambiguous. The question of which way of life is better was to plague Ibsen throughout the middle period of his work; in the social plays that are the focus of this book, he constantly shifts the spotlight from one type to the other, seeking the answer he was unable to find in his own personal life.

Ibsen's next two plays after *Peer Gynt* were still written in the Romantic style. *The League of Youth* (1869) is a satirical work principally interesting, as we shall see, as a kind of first draft for *An Enemy of the People. The Emperor and Galilean* (1873) is Ibsen's longest and most ambitious work, embodying as it does a whole theory of Western civilization. Although Ibsen often referred to it as his most positive and clear work, it is in many ways the most disappointing. The Emperor of the title is Julian the Apostate, the last pagan emperor of Rome, who attempted unsuccessfully to suppress Christianity and restore paganism as the official religion of the Empire. The Galilean, of course, is Christ, or rather Christianity, which Ibsen characterizes as cold and repressive; there is thus a neat, all too easy equation of Christianity with the ethical life and paganism with the aesthetic.

In Ibsen's version of the story, Julian tries to found a religion that will not merely restore traditional paganism, but also transcend both it and Christianity. Julian's friend and mentor, the philosopher Maximus, relates this to the political history of Rome:

> There are three empires. . . . that empire which was founded on the tree of knowledge; then that empire which was founded on the tree of the cross. . . . The third is the empire of the great mystery, the empire which shall be founded on the tree of knowledge and the tree of the cross together.[18]

But Julian is unsuccessful in his attempt to found this "empire of the great mystery," which corresponds to Kierkegaard's religious stage. Murdered by a Christian, Julian dies at dawn, like Peer Gynt and also Osvald in *Ghosts* (although unlike theirs, Julian's death is real, rather than an ambiguous reversion to childhood).

The play is an attack on the nineteenth-century bourgeoisie, with their repressed life style, a common subject in the literature of the period, as in Matthew Arnold's poem "The Buried Life." But the result is all too much like what one imagines Ejlert Løvborg's book of history to be in *Hedda Gabler,* grandiosely conceived, turgidly executed, and boring to read. The play lacks the compressed intensity of *Brand* and the wild humor of *Peer Gynt;* Ibsen was merely repeating the same ideas in a more explicit, and hence more dry and undramatic, way. A better solution was to rework the material through the conventions of a new theatrical form that was rapidly gaining popularity—realism.

Pillars of Society, completed in 1877, was Ibsen's first attempt at the new realistic style. Like *Emperor and Galilean,* it suffers from dramatic clumsiness, including what Charles R. Lyons has described as the "mechanical conversion" of the hero at the end.[19] But with his next three plays—*A Doll House* (1879), *Ghosts* (1881), and *An Enemy of the People* (1882)—Ibsen reached his stride. (Like most great playwrights, Ibsen was always a slow learner.) These plays established his reputation in Europe, as *Brand* and *Peer Gynt* had established it in Norway. All have contemporary, interior settings, taking advantage of the recently developed box set; they are filled with the mundane details of everyday life; the heroes are bourgeois; and, unfortunately for Ibsen's reputation as it turned out in the long run, all deal with social problems. *Pillars of Society* had dealt with "floating coffins" (unsafe ships financed by unscrupulous merchants in order to gain larger profits); *A Doll House* touches on women's rights and free love (in the subplot of Krogstad and Mrs. Linde); *Ghosts* is concerned with the effects of syphilis; *An Enemy of the People* deals with water pollution and freedom of speech. But these topics are never the plays' total meanings. Ibsen is always more concerned with his particular characters' handling of the problem, than with the problem by itself. It is important to remember that Ibsen was a middle-aged, experienced playwright by this time—*Pillars of Society,* for example, was his *fifteenth* play, written when he was forty-nine. The Romantic tradition in drama, with its tendency to idealize characters, and to see social problems in terms of personal choices, never left him. Specifically, as I shall attempt to show, it is still possible to explicate the characters in the social plays according to Kierkegaard's levels; to explicate dramatic elements like scenic background, setting, properties, and verbal imagery in similar terms; and even to see repeats of the actual devices of *Brand* and *Peer Gynt,* such as the North-South polarity, the opposition of warmth and light to coldness and darkness, and the use of animal images. Ibsen's social plays, then, represent the reworking of his earlier material into new forms; they are a secularization or demythologizing of the Romantic.

4/The Ethical Leap: *A Doll House*

A Doll House is still the best known of Ibsen's plays. Although Ibsen later disclaimed any connection with the Feminist movement, insisting that the play was concerned with human rights and not merely with women's rights,[1] and despite subsequent books and articles pointing out that issues like votes for women or equal job opportunity are never even mentioned in the play, *A Doll House* remains famous for its Feminism. A recent edition of the play attempted to cash in on the Women's Liberation movement by advertizing, "Women's rights had a champion 100 years ago."[2] There is of course an element of truth in this; one did not write a play in 1879 about a woman's leaving her husband and children without at least a minimal interest in women's rights. Even today, with divorce much more common than it was a hundred years ago, women rarely walk out on their *children*.

Nevertheless, it will not do to treat *A Doll House* as a mere thesis play or social tract. As English professors are forever telling their freshmen, one must not extract any single element from a literary work and consider it out of context. And the dramatic context of Ibsen's middle plays is never that of mass movements. Ibsen himself was never a member of a political party or social improvement society of any sort; in fact, the very idea of democratic movements is scornfully satirized in *An Enemy of the People*. The context of these plays is always that of the individual, faced with monumental challenge. When Mrs. Linde, in the third act,

89

asks Krogstad to take her home with him so that they can live together, it may be considered as a plea for "free love"; but that phrase itself is never used, and no generalizations from Mrs. Linde's choice are ever put into the mouths of the characters. Regardless of what inferences the reader or audience member wishes to draw, the scene's focus remains on Mrs. Linde herself.

The critical history of the play has been most unfortunate; valued first for the wrong reasons, it was later denigrated on the same grounds. The play's reputation for Feminism was first established—indeed, championed—in the English-speaking world by William Archer and Bernard Shaw. Shaw's *Quintessence of Ibsenism,* published in 1891, did much of the damage. As a matter of fact, Shaw's book still reads very well as an *introduction* to Ibsen. Shaw is not insensitive to Ibsen's poetic values, and he generally treats the plays as dramatic works, not tracts. But Ibsen's plays had been known for only three years in England when the book was written, and they had never been given proper production. As a result, Shaw, with his own definite political bias, and under the influence of Archer's poor translations and incorrect attitudes toward the plays, overstresses Ibsen as a social reformer, and in particular insists over and over that Ibsen was an anti-idealist, which Ibsen *never* completely was, not even in *The Wild Duck.* At any rate, what was meant to be the first word on Ibsen came to be taken as the last word; for decades, until the publication of M. C. Bradbrook's *Ibsen the Norwegian* in 1946, Shaw's view went unmodified in the English-speaking world. *A Doll House* was championed as a masterpiece of realism and Feminism; then, with the passage of time, it came to be ridiculed on exactly the same grounds. As realism became passé, *A Doll House* was passed off as being shallow and journalistic. With the gaining of new rights for women in the 1920s, it was criticized in addition for being

THE ETHICAL LEAP/91

outdated—a premature judgment, as subsequent events have proved.

Furthermore, as critics began to point out, even its much-touted realism is often clumsy and *un*natural. The characterization of Krogstad, for example, is that of a villain out of the cheapest melodrama, and his sudden conversion at the end of the play is a bit of sentimentality like the conversion of Consul Bernick at the end of *Pillars of Society,* a weakly motivated contrivance. The trip south to save Helmer's life, which caused all the trouble in the first place, is ridiculously unscientific—as if a vacation on the Mediterranean could have transformed a dying man into the healthy, vigorous individual we actually see when the play begins. Dr. Rank, the brooding, dying doctor, is an obvious death symbol, and symbols are something that realism was supposed to have got rid of. Worst of all, Nora's famous decision to leave is itself poorly motivated; she has been characterized until then as frivolous and naive, and to have her suddenly walk out on her husband, and especially on her children, after a single argument, is simply too much to believe. *A Doll House* contains, moreover, all the major elements of the nineteenth-century Well-made Play. Shaw, who had ridiculed such elements by calling them "Sardoodledom," failed to note such standard contrivances here as the late point of attack, necessitating endless exposition; the suppressed secret of the forgery; the obvious device of Krogstad's letter; the obligatory scene, or *scène à faire,* at the end of the play, in which Nora and Helmer confront each other and Nora achieves her victory. This is realism of the most mechanical sort.

Thus, critics came to attack the play both for being too realistic and for not being realistic enough. But all the apparent flaws in the play disappear if one accepts this paradox not as a defect but rather as an advantage. If we stop viewing *A Doll House* solely in realistic terms and accept its underlying, contrapuntal Romanticism, even its Feminism becomes clear—what is that but the "secularization" of the idealized woman of Romantic drama, starting with Margaret in Goethe's *Faust* and continuing through Agnes and Solveig in Ibsen's own *Brand* and *Peer Gynt?* Ibsen, like all the great realistic dramatists whose plays have lasted, was never interested in merely showing real life for its own sake (if such a thing is even possible); his plays should never be judged, positively or negatively, in simple mimetic terms. What realism did for Ibsen was to provide him with new external forms—the everyday objects and events of contemporary bourgeois life—from which to fabricate his symbolism. House, money, food, marriage, work, children—all took on the symbolic and mythical significance that Ibsen had formerly discovered in mountains, trolls, fantastic journeys, legendary animals, and weird creatures; and a door slam now served where an avalanche had been required before.

When viewed on a purely symbolic level, the play is clearly seen as full of grace and power. Dr. Rank as a death symbol is merely one in a whole complex of symbols. The play's very title is symbolic; like all of Ibsen's box sets, this house stands for the imprisoned life of the characters who live in it. Helmer's trip to recover his health is indeed clumsy, in realistic terms, but as we have seen in *Brand* and *Peer Gynt,* trips south for Ibsen had an almost magical significance. The North-South polarity continues strongly in all the plays of Ibsen's middle period (which were, in fact, written in Italy and southern Germany). In *A Doll House,* the South is associated with warmth and vitality, with Nora's love for Helmer, with the Tarantella; it contrasts with the cold gloom of Norway, Helmer's and Dr. Rank's diseases, and Helmer's stuffiness. Finally, Nora's leaving her children, difficult to imagine in a real-life bourgeois woman, is an echo of the *Kindermord* theme of the earlier plays, and also exists to enhance the magnitude of Nora's choice. Nora's decision must be sudden and extreme because of Kierkegaard's concept of the leap as something drastic; Ibsen is not writing about a "typical" woman responding to social and psychological forces, but about an exceptional one making a free, self-transforming decision. When Nora slams the door, she is not only rejecting her obtuse husband (which would certainly be courageous in terms of the social standards of the time, but which might also be viewed as mere selfishness on her part), she is making a *sacrifice*. The whole point of the play is that it is the rare individual who can give up love for duty, who can see duty to a personal ideal as transcending even the ostensibly sacred bond between mother and child. Of course, such a person might actually exist—it even appears that Nora was based on a real-life woman[3]—but unlike the more ordinary realistic playwrights, Ibsen was primarily concerned with exceptional cases.

But despite Nora's being an exceptional, free-willed character, her characterization is also treated symbolically. The play begins with her entrance; she comes in humming and carrying Christmas gifts for her children. A delivery boy follows with a Christmas tree. Nora pays him, adding a large tip (which she can hardly afford, we soon discover). As soon as he leaves, she reaches into her pocket for some macaroons, which she eats greedily. Hearing her moving about, her husband, Helmer, calls to her from his study, "Is that my little lark twittering out there?" (p. 125). He is in the habit, it appears, of calling her by the names of small animals as terms of endearment; he later repeatedly calls her a bird, a squirrel, a dove, a lark. Nora's love of music, her extravagance, her appetite, her association with animals, are all strongly reminiscent of Peer Gynt, as are her love of family (she dissembled to protect her dying father from anguish, as Peer did to comfort his dying mother in the scene where he pretends to drive her to heaven), her trip South, her ability to lie unselfconsciously, her sexuality, her dancing the Tarantella. She is firmly established as an aesthetic character.

Helmer, by contrast, is shown through the first two acts of the play as strongly ethical. If Nora is a bourgeois Peer Gynt, he is a bourgeois Brand. Nora is particularly impressed with his high moral character:

> Being a lawyer is such an uncertain living, you know, especially if one won't touch any cases that aren't clean and decent. And of course Torvald would never do that. (P. 131)

They have had to live frugally as a result of Helmer's ethics, which necessitated the loan with the forged signature when Helmer's illness required the trip South. Helmer himself would never have gone into debt:

> No debts! Never borrow! Something of freedom's lost—and something of beauty too—from a home that's founded on borrowing and debt. (P. 126)

Like Brand, he has a natural bent for preaching morals—to others. He turns every scene with Nora, until the final one, into a little moral lesson, against debt, against extravagance, against lying, against hypocrisy. But although he seems a bit of a prig, we do not suspect (nor does Nora) that his morality is a façade. When he finally learns of Nora's forged note, he at first acts true to form:

> I should have suspected something of the kind. I should have known. All your father's flimsy values—Be still! All your father's flimsy values have come out in you. No religion, no morals, no sense of duty. (P. 187)

This is just the sort of thing Nora expected. She accepts it calmly, and is even resigned to committing suicide by jumping into the river (reminiscent of Peer Gynt's plunge into the sea, as well as his threatened end in the melting pot). But almost immediately Helmer's façade crumbles. It turns out that he is more concerned with his own career than with Nora's moral character:

> Now you've wrecked all my happiness—ruined my whole future. Oh, it's awful to think of. I'm in a cheap little grafter's hands; he can do anything he wants with me, ask for anything, play with me like a puppet—and I can't breathe a word. I'll be swept down miserably into the depths on account of a featherbrained woman. (Pp. 187-88)

The irony is that he is "swept down miserably into the depths" not socially but morally. The word *puppet* is not in the original Norwegian, but it is appropriate at this point: now *he* is the "doll" of the house. His moral downfall parallels Nora's moral rise, although in Nora's case it is a genuine change while in his it is merely an unmasking; he has been a hypocrite all along.

A new letter suddenly arrives from Krogstad. Enclosing the forged note, he announces that he is ashamed of his former ways, and is turning over a new leaf. Helmer's reaction exposes further his own moral weakness—he tears up both letters and the note, and burns them, delighted that the whole affair has blown over and that his life can return to normal. The moment is extremely theatrical, in a miniature way reminiscent of Brand just before the avalanche, or of Peer Gynt dying in Solveig's arms as the sun rises: the papers burn, the little glow spreading through the room, while a "frozen look" (p. 107) comes over Nora's face; fire and ice. Ibsen likes to intensify the climaxes of his plays with lighting effects, and this moment is the true climax of the play. It is often overlooked in reading or underplayed in performance because of the famous "discussion scene" that follows, but the discussion is only the continuation of what has already happened— the vast yet almost instantaneous transformation of Nora, precipitated by the equally sudden change, in the opposite direction, of her husband. As a matter of fact, the dialogue in that scene does not really qualify as "discussion"; it is more a lengthy sermon on Nora's part, with pathetic attempts at interruption from Helmer:

> NORA. I believe that, before all else, I'm a human being, no less than you—or anyway, I ought to try to become one. I know the majority thinks you're right, Torvald, and plenty of books agree with you, too. But I can't go on believing what the majority says, or what's written in books. I have to think over these things myself and try to understand them.
> HELMER. Why can't you understand your place in your own home? On a point like that, isn't there one everlasting guide you can turn to? Where's your religion?
> NORA. Oh, Torvald, I'm really not sure what religion is.
> HELMER. What—? (P. 193)

Nora has become like Brand, skeptical of the masses and their simplistic, self-serving religion, while Helmer has become an enfeebled version of Brand's Mayor, able to challenge his wife only with half-hearted, unfelt questions.

Of equal importance to the "discussion" is the action that accompanies it. Nora changes from her dancing-girl costume (a souvenir of the trip to Italy) into regular clothes, symbolizing her inner change in character from the aesthetic to the ethical. She then continues to preach to Helmer, as he used to preach to her, telling him solemnly that "right from our first acquaintance, we've never exchanged a serious word on any serious thing" (p. 190), that she has been a doll-wife to him, that she now feels a duty to herself to find what is morally genuine in life. Helmer's words, by contrast, are now all of love, family, children—Nora's former obsessions. But he realizes that it is of no use, echoing *Brand* with the forlorn phrase, "There's a gulf that's opened between us" (p. 195), a gulf that is further emphasized by the slammed door at the end.

Thus, Helmer and Nora reflect each other in reverse, both before and after Nora's change. In fact, all the characters in the play can once again be arranged in a Kierkegaardian scheme, reinforcing and contrasting one another:

AESTHETIC	Ironic	ETHICAL
Nora (Acts 1, 2, beginning of 3)	⟶	Nora (end of 3)
Helmer (end of 3)	⟵ (Helmer throughout)	Helmer (1, 2, beginning of 3)
Krogstad (1, 2, beginning of 3)	⟶	Krogstad (end of 3)
The Helmer children		
Dr. Rank (middle of 2, 3)	⟵	Dr. Rank (1, beginning of 2)
Mrs. Linde (before play)	⟶	Mrs. Linde (during play)
Delivery Boy		
Maids		
Nora's father (dead)		

The numerous arrows show how much this is a play about change. Helmer, as can be seen, is a special case, since he does not really change; his true character is revealed at the end, but he is actually at the hypocritical, intermediate, ironic level throughout. We see the ethical side of him through the first two-and-a-half acts, and the aesthetic side at the end.

This scheme also clarifies the position of Krogstad. His transformation can indeed be considered stagy, but this is because his transformation, like Nora's, is so abrupt and weakly motivated. It must thus again be considered an internal choice rather than a change resulting from external forces. He is a "reflector" of Nora, and his change reflects hers. His transformation comes at a crucial point in his life, when he is under the pressure of losing his job and his carefully restored reputation, and it is directly triggered by Mrs. Linde's offer to marry him. But it is still his own choice to reform; in fact, Mrs. Linde has to talk him into *not* taking back his letter to Helmer. Like Nora, Krogstad makes a sudden leap from the aesthetic life to the ethical. Like her, he has been self-seeking, amoral, ready to go to any extreme to protect his family. The parallel is stressed in Act 2, when Nora pleads with him to consider her children, to which he replies, "Did you or your husband ever think of mine?" (p. 168). After his change, he becomes dutiful, confident, and even moralistic; despite his love for Mrs. Linde, he can still accuse her of having set the whole thing up:

> KROGSTAD *(looks at her searchingly)*. Is that the meaning of it, then? You'll save your friend at any price. Tell me straight out. Is that it? (P. 179)

This brief flash of moral rectitude (which quickly fades in this case) has an ugly, ruthless quality that recalls Brand in his worst moments, and foreshadows a similar hardness in Nora at the end. The dramatic function of Krogstad's transformation, then, is to mirror Nora's transformation. The situation is like plot and subplot in Shakespeare, one of Ibsen's most important literary influences. And, like so many of the apparent flaws in Shakespeare, Krogstad's quick change is a flaw only if we insist on looking at the play in terms of modern psychology; viewed symbolically, the change is not flawed at all, but clear, powerful, and even necessary.

The situation of Mrs. Linde also parallels that of Nora.

The first connection between the two is in the fact that she is a former schoolmate of Nora's; they are of the same age, sex, class, and social background. In Mrs. Linde's first scene with Nora (p. 133) we learn that since the last time the two were together Mrs. Linde married a man she did not really love for the sake of his money—in other words, she too had her "doll house." After the death of her husband, however, she changed drastically, taking charge of her mother and young brothers, working for her living, and generally leading an independent life. Nora does not even recognize her old friend when she arrives, because she has become so different (p. 130). In fact, she has become so obsessed with living for duty that now that her mother has died and her brothers have grown up she is searching for new burdens; when Nora remarks that she must at last feel free of care and obligation, Mrs. Linde replies, "No—only unspeakably empty. Nothing to live for now" (p. 133). Clearly, Mrs. Linde has already made the ethical leap that Nora will soon take; she has, in Kierkegaard's words, "clad herself in duty," as an expression of her inmost nature.

Mrs. Linde is thus one of Ibsen's unexpected visitors from the past—like Ejnar in *Brand*—who reflect the main character. More specifically, she provides a direct inspiration for Nora's eventual change, by proving to Nora that a woman can function on her own. Similarly, it is Mrs. Linde who provides the inspiration for Krogstad's transformation at the end: when he sees that there is indeed one selfless person in a world that he has up to then considered entirely venal, he decides to make the ethical leap himself. The characterization of Mrs. Linde thus functions dramatically on two levels—indirectly, as a parallel to the transformation of Nora, and directly, as a catalyst for the transformations of both Nora and Krogstad. She is also interesting as one of the few ethical characters in Ibsen's plays who are shown to be unequivocally good. She thus tends to intensify the audience's attitude toward Nora's decision to leave, making seem valid what might have otherwise easily seemed dubious. We know that Nora *must* change because Mrs. Linde says she must, and we have come to accept her judgments in the play; and we know that Nora *can* succeed in the cold world outside her doll house, because Mrs. Linde has already shown it to be possible.

It is interesting also to compare the attitudes of the two women toward sexual love. There are two love scenes in the play (or three if you count the abortive one between Torvald and Nora in Act 3). In the second act, Nora flirts with Doctor Rank because she thinks, vaguely, that he might be able to come up with some money to pay off Krogstad. Actually, Krogstad does not want to keep his little job at the bank for the money (he could easily make more by loansharking), but rather for respectability. It is typical of Nora's mindlessness, however, that when she finds herself in trouble she does not analyze the problem rationally but rather uses her feminine charm on the first likely man to come along. The box of costumes she has been sorting for the masquerade provides her with a convenient prop:

> NORA. Dr. Rank, sit over here and I'll show you something.
> RANK. *(sitting).* What's that?
> NORA. Look here. Look.
> RANK. Silk stockings.
> NORA. Flesh-colored. Aren't they lovely? Now it's so dark here, but tomorrow—No, no, no, just look at the feet. Oh well, you might as well look at the rest.
> RANK. Hm—
> NORA. Why do you look so critical? Don't you believe they'll fit?
> RANK. I've never had any chance to form an opinion on that.

NORA *(glancing at him a moment).* Shame on you. *(Hits him lightly on the ear with the stockings.)* That's for you. (P. 164)

Nora is brought up sharply, however, when her flirtation brings from Doctor Rank the startling assertion that he is in love with her, and always has been. Phony emotion has brought on real emotion. Nora cannot stand such honesty in love, and puts a quick end to the little game, calling for the maid to bring in a lamp, and bitterly chiding the doctor not for loving her but, significantly, because "you came out and told me" (p. 165). Sex for Nora is thus shown to be a charade, a means to an end—or a masquerade, like the one where she will dance the Tarantella that so excites her husband. We thus see in this indirect way that the whole sexual relation between Nora and her husband is dishonest. They do not love each other; they do not even really desire each other; they *play* with each other, like dolls. Their whole marriage is a masquerade.

In contrast with this is the love scene between Mrs. Linde and Krogstad at the beginning of Act 3. Mrs. Linde does not flirt. Her language remains blunt, and she comes right out and offers herself to Krogstad, saying "take me home" without even a mention of the word *marriage*. This was certainly a startling thing for a woman of the time; the only reason that the shock of it has generally gone unnoticed is that it is overshadowed by the greater shock later of Nora's walking out on Helmer. But for all her bluntness, Mrs. Linde is not unemotional. Her offer is not a calculating attempt to manipulate Krogstad (as Nora's was with Dr. Rank), nor a cold attempt to "improve" him, but a genuine expression of love:

MRS. LINDE. Nils, if only we two shipwrecked people could reach across to each other.
KROGSTAD. What are you saying?
MRS. LINDE. Two on one wreck are at least better off than each on his own.

KROGSTAD. Kristine!
MRS. LINDE. Why do you think I came into town? (P. 178)

This is marriage as described by Kierkegaard in his ethical persona: "the downright seriousness of life, and yet it is not cold, uncomely, unerotic, unpoetic."[4] Mrs. Linde's offer combines duty and love; her marriage to Krogstad will have the validity that the Helmers' lacks, despite its unconventionality. (It is not even clear whether there will be a marriage ceremony.) This scene shows that Ibsen was not opposed to *all* marriage, but only marriages that had no ethical significance, that lacked, to use Kierkegaard's words, "seriousness." It also shows that it is genuinely possible that the Helmers may be reunited again in the future; "the greatest miracle"—a rebirth into the ethical life—may one day happen to Helmer as it happens here to Krogstad.

Dr. Rank is a more minor character than Nora, Helmer, Mrs. Linde, or Krogstad, but he must not be dismissed as merely emblematic of death. He, like Mrs. Linde, is an ethical character: he helps people through his profession (including Helmer when he was ill), as well as offering sympathy and advice. He is tough, open, sincere. His honest declaration of love for Nora in the second act parallels Mrs. Linde's similar declaration of love for Krogstad in the third. Yet there are elements in his characterization that contrast meaningfully with that of Mrs. Linde. The reason he seems to be a death symbol is that, like Ejnar in *Brand,* he is a little in love with death—announcing it with a calling card marked with a black cross, hiding himself out in his bedroom. The subject of his own death holds a lurid fascination for him, as he speaks of how "within a month I'll probably be laid out and rotting in the churchyard" (p. 162). For Rank, then, the realization of physical death is the kind of crisis that Nora faces when she realizes that her husband is not the paragon she believed him to be, or the crisis that Helmer himself faces when he receives Krogstad's letter. Rank reacts to the crisis by trying to reembrace the aesthetic life; he is bitter that he is suffering for his father's sins (his disease is apparently inherited syphilis) yet "never shared the fun" (p. 163). He therefore tries to grab as much fun as he can—attempting to make love to Nora, going to parties, drinking, smoking fine cigars, and finally (in a significant animal image) hiding himself away "like a wounded animal" (p. 186). But it does not work. Unlike Mrs. Linde, who easily incorporates love and warmth into her ethical life, the attempt of this fine man to go out in a blaze of sensuality is merely ugly and pathetic. In other words, it is a *fall*, which parallels the similar moral fall of his friend Helmer.

The analysis so far makes an important point about Ibsen's social drama: just as it is never a profession of a simple social thesis, so too is it not merely the depiction of a single hero or heroine. *A Doll House* is a study of the relation between the aesthetic and ethical levels of life, of the way in which people, in moments of crisis, choose one or the other or attempt to cling to both. The heroine undergoes such a change in *A Doll House,* but that is only one aspect of the play. In total, the play is actually an intricately connected complex of characters and ideas; the characters in particular not only relate to one another directly, but also contrast with and parallel each other symbolically. Ibsen's plays have the "spatial" quality of the same sort that G. Wilson Knight has described about Shakespeare's:

> A Shakespearian tragedy is set spatially as well as temporally in the mind. By this I mean that there are throughout the play a set of correspondences which

relate to each other independently of the time-sequence which is the story: such are the intuition-intelligence opposition active within and across *Troilus and Cressida,* the death-theme in *Hamlet,* the nightmare evil of *Macbeth.*[5]

Similarly, the aesthetic-ethical opposition is "active within and across" *A Doll House.* Nora's ethical leap has "correspondences" to the changes in Helmer, Mrs. Linde, Krogstad, and Dr. Rank. The play is externally a realistic study of a woman's leaving her husband, but internally a complex of poetic associations that leap across the direct and "scientific" causal relationships to make abstract and symbolic points. In other words, the play is a work of art rather than a case study.

Nor are the correspondences in the play limited to the major characters. Ibsen's control of small detail here is again as consistent, and as striking, as that of Shakespeare. Consider, for example, the Helmer children: they appear only briefly, and as a result, since children are difficult to work with onstage, they have often been cut from performance. It seems a simple matter to leave them out—when Helmer, Dr. Rank, and Mrs. Linde exit in the middle of Act 1, instead of having the children enter, the director can leave Nora alone onstage (perhaps to do a bit of embroidery, as she later does when she is alone) for a few moments until Krogstad enters. The surface plot is then not damaged a bit; the children's scene provides no essential exposition, and there are enough references to children at other times to establish the fact that Nora is a mother. But unless the audience actually sees the scene with the children, it loses important emotional and symbolic values associated with them. For one thing, the scene strongly establishes Nora's love for her children, so that when she walks out on them at the end, the audience has a vivid sense of what she is giving up. But the specific details of the scene are important as well. The initial talk is all about the children's *playing* outside—pulling each other on the sled, throwing snowballs—which leads Nora to say, "Oh, if I'd only been there" (p. 143). Nora dances with the children, and then engages them in a game of hide-and-seek, which is interrupted by Krogstad's entrance. The meaning is clear: Nora treats her children as if she were one of them. And we see none of the more austere aspects of childhood—discipline, schoolwork, fear, hostility, disease. Their life appears to be all play. There is mention of a "big black dog" seen outside, an animal image that reinforces our sense of a lower level of existence; and most important, Nora twice refers to her children as "doll babies." This is a doll house in which both she and the children are dolls. Nora loves her children, but it is a juvenile, unserious form of love that is ultimately as bad for them as it is for her.

This kind of juvenile love is reflected in another minor character, the nursemaid Anne-Marie. There are actually two maids in the Helmer household, and for some reason both have French names—Anne-Marie and Helene. Perhaps it was fashionable at the time in Norway to have French maids, but no logical justification is ever spelled out. On the other hand, they too serve a symbolic purpose, their exotic names echoing the "southern" world of the aesthetic life that contrasts so often in Ibsen's plays with the austere ethical world of Norway. We do not learn anything about Helene, but Anne-Marie's story, told briefly at the beginning of Act 2, turns out to be interesting: she had had an illegitimate child, whom she left years ago when she became Nora's nurse; now, of course, she is nurse to Nora's children. Anne-Marie's having left her child provides the audience with the first hint that Nora might leave her own children:

> NORA. You old Anne-Marie, you were a good mother for me when I was little.
> ANNE-MARIE. Poor little Nora, with no other mother but me.
> NORA. And if the babies didn't have one, then I know that you'd—What silly talk! (P. 155)

Nora, however, is thinking at this point not of walking out on Helmer, but of suicide, and Anne-Marie's experience turns out to be different from Nora's in a significant respect. Anne-Marie did not leave her child out of a sense of duty, but simply out of necessity:

> NORA. How could you ever have the heart to give your child over to strangers?
> ANNE-MARIE. But I had to, you know, to become little Nora's nurse.
> NORA. Yes, but how could you *do* it?
> ANNE-MARIE. When I could get such a good place? A girl who's poor and who's gotten in trouble is glad enough for that. Because that slippery fish, he didn't do a thing for me, you know. (P. 155)

Anne-Marie has made no ethical leap, but rather continues to live the aesthetic life. This is reinforced by her attitude toward her child, whom she never even sees, and from whom she has heard only twice, "both when she was confirmed and when she was married" (p. 155). Anne-Marie's love for children, like Nora's, is juvenile or animal-like. She loves them deeply when they are actually there, and forgets them when they are not; she has shifted easily from her own child to Nora, and then from Nora to Nora's children, and no doubt would shift just as easily to someone else's children if it should become necessary. It recalls Peer Gynt's love for his mother, which was real enough when she was alive but is forgotten the instant she is dead. The actual things we see or hear of Anne-Marie's doing in the household are all of the aesthetic rather than ethical sort: she goes out playing with the children, drinks a cup of cocoa, brings out masquerade clothes. When the children come running into the living room, she makes no attempt to restrain or reprimand them. She is obviously not the sort of nursemaid who disciplines the children very much or teaches them anything. Anne-Marie represents an attitude toward motherhood that Nora must transcend.

Two other characters remain in the play, one of whom appears only briefly—the Delivery Boy—and the other who does not appear at all—Nora's dead father. The Delivery Boy brings in the Christmas tree at the beginning. Although his scene is short, it has considerably more impact in performance than appears at first glance on the page:

> NORA. Hide the tree well, Helene. The children mustn't get a glimpse of it till this evening, after it's trimmed. *(To the Delivery Boy, taking out her purse.)* How much?
> DELIVERY BOY. Fifty, ma'am.
> NORA. There's a crown. No, keep the change. *(The boy thanks her and leaves.)* (P. 125)

The tree, of course, immediately establishes an air of festivity, as do the presents Nora brings in and the fact that she is "humming happily to herself." The fact that he is a boy foreshadows the importance of children in this play, and Nora's overtipping him (despite her need for frugality) establishes her attitude toward children. Their little shared moment of delight as the boy takes the huge tip can have real force if played well by good actors.

Nora's father was the immediate cause of all Nora's trouble. It was his name she forged, since he was dying at the time she needed the money. Lacking any sense of business procedures, she foolishly dated the note after her father's death. But Ibsen does not leave Nora's father as a mere plot device. There are several descriptions of his character. In the opening scene, Helmer suggests that Nora has inherited his characteristics:

> You're an odd little one. Exactly the way your father was. You're never at a loss for scaring up money; but the moment you have it, it runs right out through your fingers; you never know what you've done with it. Well, one takes you as you are. It's deep in your blood. Yes, these things are hereditary, Nora. (P. 128)

Helmer repeats his attitude toward Nora's father twice more. In the second act, when Nora urges him to reinstate Krogstad, because she fears that Helmer will be slandered in the papers the way her father was over some shady dealings, Helmer replies:

> My dear Nora, there's a notable difference between your father and me. Your father's official career was hardly above reproach. But mine is. (P. 160)

Finally, in the last act, when Helmer has found out about the forged note and is berating Nora, he says:

> Oh, quit posing. Your father had a mess of those speeches too. (P. 188)

Two important things are thus established by Helmer about Nora and her father: first, that he too was of the aesthetic type, amoral, a spendthrift, a liar. Second, Helmer insists that Nora has inherited her father's characteristics. At the same time, as I have already noted, Nora was raised by her nursemaid, Anne-Marie, and no doubt received her attitudes toward motherhood, and life in general, from her. In realistic terms, Nora's behavior is thus completely "caused"; she has been shaped into what she is both by heredity and by upbringing. This makes her decision to leave all the more impressive—she leaps right out of the deterministic, realistic framework that Ibsen has carefully created for her, to become a genuinely heroic character. (It is interesting that when Nora announces her decision to leave, Helmer goes on looking for realistic "causes," insisting that "you're sick; you've got a fever" [p. 193].) Both Anne-Marie and Nora's father, although minor characters (we do not see her father, and never even learn his name), serve to root Nora in the aesthetic life, making her escape from it all the more dramatic.

This paradox of free-willed characters in a deterministic world is the key to the understanding of Ibsen's use of the Well-made Play form. The Well-made Play, a precursor of realism, involves a mechanical approach to dramaturgy in which every element in a play is connected and "caused." The hero in Scribe's *A Glass of Water* says:

> States are subjugated or controlled by heroes, by great men; but these great men are themselves slaves to their passions, their whims, their vanities . . . that is, by whatever is small and mean in this world. Perhaps you do not know that a window in the Château Trianon, criticized by Louis XIV and defended by Louvois, was responsible for the war which involves Europe at the present moment. It is to the wounded vanity of a courtesan that a kingdom owes its disasters; perhaps to so small a cause as that the king absent-mindedly failed to answer her over the breakfast table.[6]

Here is expressed the philosophy behind the Well-made Play; this philosophy is not so scientific as the realistic playwrights like Strindberg were later to make it, but it is equally deterministic. Events are controlled by passions, whims, and vanities, by windows and courtesans and glasses of water. The smallness of these elements reflects a belief in the importance of *background*. Playwrights like Scribe of course did not invent causality in drama, but by moving causes from the foreground of personal choice to the background of minor events, outside the characters' direct control, they generated a sense of a deterministic world in which characters are ruled by abstract forces. Such forces might well be expressed through major events in addition to minor ones, but the stressing of minutiae creates a feeling that the characters are utterly helpless. Major causes can be confronted and, possibly, counteracted; minor ones in the background cannot even be fully known.

A Doll House is certainly influenced by the Well-made Play; it is full of small but significant causes, like the forged note (revealed because of a minor discrepancy in the date), Krogstad's letter, Dr. Rank's calling cards, Mrs. Linde's chance return to town and her coincidental taking over of the very job that had been Krogstad's. But unlike in *A Glass of Water,* the machinery in *A Doll House* does not have much to do with what is fundamentally going on in the play, which is Nora's change and the parallel changes in other characters. Ibsen seems even to get bored with all the secrets and letters, and the machinations of the villain Krogstad, because just at the crucial point when Krogstad is at last persuaded by Mrs. Linde to take back the incriminating letter that has been lying ominously in the mailbox for the past day and a half, Ibsen suddenly drops the whole thing. Mrs. Linde changes her mind, tells Krogstad not to take back the letter, and explains:

> Helmer's got to learn everything; this dreadful secret has to be aired; those two have to come to a full understanding; all these lies and evasions can't go on. (P. 179)

Thus, Nora's decision to leave her husband does *not* arise from the manipulations of the plot. Mrs. Linde makes a conscious *choice* to let Helmer in on the secret of Nora's forgery. The letter is merely Mrs. Linde's means to her end at that point; if for some reason the letter were destroyed, or Nora were able to persuade Helmer not to open it (as she tries to do), we know that Mrs. Linde would find some other way of informing Helmer. If *A Doll House* were an unalloyed Well-made Play in the style of Scribe or Sardou, this would be a serious flaw—that is, it would be absolutely necessary that the letter, like Scribe's glass of water or Sardou's piece of paper, be the small but essential piece of machinery that brings on the denouement. But when the denouement does arrive in *A Doll House,* we are not even interested in the machinery any more—if we ever were. Ibsen's characters have transcended it.

Furthermore, the denouement itself is not what we would expect in a Well-made Play. The obligatory scene at the end is supposed to be a confrontation between the hero (or heroine) and the villain, which means in this case between Nora and Krogstad. They have already had such confrontations in Acts 1 and 2, and we would expect (if we were foolish enough to take this as a hack play) that the ending would be a showdown between the two. Instead, Krogstad suddenly converts into a decent person, and Helmer, who has seemed moral and considerate all along, is given the position of confronting Nora in the final scene, turning out to be the *true* villain of the piece. Again, Ibsen has set his characters in a rigid plot framework, and then allowed them to escape it; what had seemed determined has become free willed. And it is precisely this paradox that makes the play interesting, preventing it from being merely an example of stock nineteenth-century commercial drama. The play is "flawed," but its flaw is what makes it original and striking.

Ibsen's treatment of small detail, while also drawn from the Well-made Play, again transcends the form. Theatrical elements such as costume, properties, and setting are treated in the same symbolic way as is characterization.

Much of this, again, is far more noticeable in performance than on the page, unless one takes special care to look for it. Many critics have noticed the significance of Nora's change of costume at the end; while Helmer is talking to her from the living room, she goes off stage and changes from her Tarantella costume to a street dress. The visual impact of this change is striking: one moment she is wearing a loose, colorful costume that exposes a good deal of her body for the Victorian period; the next moment she is completely covered up, because of the prim fashions of the time, and also because of the need for protection against the cold outside when she leaves. Equally striking, but less often noticed by the critics, are the costume changes for Helmer and Dr. Rank. In the first two acts, they wear the typical costume of the bourgeois professional in the mid-Victorian period—dark, heavy, dignified suits with tight collars and black ties. In the last act, they are in full evening dress, giving them a showy, self-glorifying look that expresses the inner change they undergo. Their dress is not precisely specified, but if the costume designer follows the fashions of the period, all kinds of extravagances are possible that are rarely found today—silk top hats, opera capes, colored waistcoats, frilly shirts, and even jewelry. It is again an example of integrated symbolism; the costumes for all three characters are fully justified by the circumstances, yet emotionally expressive as well.

The play has a very long prop list, and the props too are symbolic in their effect. Contrasted with such ethical-level items as money, letters, notes, and business papers are items associated with the aesthetic life, such as a piano, the children's gifts, Nora's macaroons, and the Christmas tree. And, in this play of changes, even some of these make significant "leaps": in the first act, we see the Christmas tree delivered, and actually see Nora decorate it. At the beginning of the second act, however, Ibsen's stage directions specify that "the Christmas tree now stands stripped of ornament, burned-down candle stubs on its ragged branches" (p. 154). Such contrasts are very noticeable in actual performance; although mentioned only once in the stage directions, they are of course a *constant* visual reminder of the transformations that are taking place in the world of the play. The festive air that Nora strove desperately to create in Act 1 has become burned-out and dead, and the stripped and ragged Christmas tree not only is an intellectual reminder of that fact, but also forms a dreary picture that makes the audience *feel* the change.

Setting is another theatrical element that Ibsen manipulates symbolically as well as realistically. There is, first of all, the setting of the play in time: it is no accident that the action takes place during the Christmas holiday. (By coincidence, the play was first produced in Norway at Christmastime, in 1879, which must have added to its forcefulness.) The ambivalent emotions that we associate with Christmas reinforce this as a play of transition. On the one hand, Christmas is a religious celebration, a time of joy, brotherhood, and generosity. On the other, it is a time of commercial greed (not so strong a hundred years ago as today, but still very much in evidence, as seen in the play by all the extravagant gifts that Nora has purchased), of false heartiness with people we detest, of hangovers and indigestion. Furthermore, in northern countries it occurs at a time when the weather is generally miserable, which is made clear in the play by the many references to the cold, dark, snowy world outside, and by the characters whom we see enter in heavy coats, hats, gloves, muffs, and scarfs. The conflicting emotions aroused by Christmastime set the play in a liminal, ambivalent world that both reflects and reinforces the frantic emotions in Nora. The emotional ambiguities of Christmas amplify the *moral* ambiguities in the Helmer family; the strain of the holidays makes the characters more apt to flare up, more apt to expose themselves, more likely to take chances, as so many characters in the play do. The strain on Nora of partying and the incessant need for shopping, for trimming the tree, for giving dinners, for practicing the Tarantella, for greeting old friends, for maintaining a jolly exterior—all at the very time she is being threatened by Krogstad—create in Nora an emotional crisis that she must finally resolve by redefining herself, by becoming a new kind of person and renouncing the old.

The liminal quality of the play's time period has a counterpart in its physical setting. There is a strong contrast between the inside and the outside, the warm, womblike living room and the cold world of ice and snow outdoors; but there is also a hallway—actually *two* hallways—through which characters must pass to get from one to the other. The setting is rather difficult to visualize from the stage directions, although it is clear and logical enough in performance: The Helmers live not in a house, but in an apartment, on the second floor of a building in a small Norwegian town. (There is another apartment upstairs, where the masked ball takes place.) There is therefore an outer hallway, which gives access to all the other apartments, and an inner hallway, within the Helmer apartment, through which people pass, after entering the front door, to get to the living room. To get from the living room to the outside, then, as mentioned earlier, a person must go through no less than *three* doors: from the living room through a door (or at least a doorway) to the inner hall; through the apartment's front door (which holds the all-important letterbox) to the outer hall; then downstairs to the main door of the apartment building, which is the one that Nora slams at the end. When Nora walks out, we thus get the feeling that she is going through some kind of rite of passage, an initiation ritual with numerous stages—doorway, hall, door, hall, stairs, and final door for her escape to the outside. This is an aspect of the play where Ibsen had free choice; he could have given the Helmers a house, or even an apartment on the ground floor, without changing the play's surface at all. Instead, he gave us a setting with numerous thresholds, recalling all those crevasses and the fjord in *Brand*, that symbolize the gaps between levels of existence. The elaborate separation between the inner and the outer world increases the polarity between them; we feel that Nora's "doll house" is a refuge from the cold, hard world outside, a safe haven—or a prison. In Kierkegaardian terms we might say that the living room represents Nora's aesthetic life, and the cold outside world the ethical life, with the complex hallway arrangement representing the liminal, "ironic" life through which she must quickly pass to go from one valid (though immature) level of existence to another. But again, this is not merely an intellectual code or set of emblems on Ibsen's part; warm rooms, cold outdoors, and labyrinthian hallways really make us *feel* alternately safe, challenged, or confused. Ibsen capitalizes on these emotional facts about human beings to reinforce the play's basic, underlying action, the movement from the aesthetic to the ethical life.

Even within the living room that forms the play's single setting, Ibsen maintains symbolically the aesthetic-ethical polarity. Although the room is a kind of womb for Nora, in the wall up left[7] there is a window to the outside through which the audience can see the ominous, snowy weather that is a constant background to all the action. Near this window Ibsen calls for a round table; it is here that the play's serious scenes take place—the final "discussion" scene is specifically placed with Nora and Helmer at the table, for example (p. 190). Diagonally opposite the window and table, in the wall down right, Ibsen calls for a stove with two armchairs and a rocking chair beside it. The stove is a focal point for emotional as well as physical warmth; when Mrs. Linde comes in, for example, Nora says:

> You're not still cold? *(Helping her.)* There now, let's get cozy here by the stove. No, the easy chair there. I'll take the rocker here. (P. 130)

Helmer refers to the stove corner in similar terms:

> And so, enough of that. *(Sitting by the stove.)* Ah, how snug and cozy it is here. (P. 150)

Finally, Nora tends to go to the stove whenever she is emotionally upset, as when Dr. Rank expresses his love for her:

> NORA *(in the hall doorway).* Helene, bring the lamp in. *(Goes over to the stove.)* Ah, dear Dr. Rank, that was really mean of you. (P. 165)

The stage directions, then, establish the stove corner as the "aesthetic" area of the room, and the window and table corner, placed as far as possible from the stove, as the "ethical" area.

Such stage directions are all the more significant when one realizes how surprisingly few such directions there are in this play; sometimes pages go by with few or no stage directions at all, even when it is clear that the characters must be moving about. Probably Ibsen, having had a good deal of practical theater experience in his youth as director of the theater at Bergen, recognized that all stages are different, and thus included only a few of the most essential stage directions to establish a pattern. Directors and actors could then adapt this pattern to the needs of a particular production. In a production in 1975 at the University of Calgary, for example, the actress spoke the following lines, referring to Nora's proposed suicide, while looking out the window, although the playscript does not explicitly say where she is supposed to be at the time:

> Never see him again. Never, never. (*Putting her shawl over her head.*) Never see the children either—them too. Never, never. Oh, the freezing black water! The depths—down— Oh, I wish it were over— He has it now; he's reading it—now. Oh no, no, not yet. Torvald, good-bye, you and the children— (P. 187)

Anyone who has worked in the theater knows that it is almost standard practice to ignore overly elaborate stage directions, as when Bernard Shaw tells us that the blue eyes of one of his characters are "just the thirty-secondth of an inch too wide open." But on the other hand, great playwrights like Shaw and Ibsen do not write stage directions at random, or just to entertain the reader; there is always an underlying metaphorical significance that the director and his actors must grasp. It is not absolutely essential that Nora deliver her suicide speech at the window, nor indeed that any specific stage direction be followed exactly as it reads in the text. What *is* important is that the symbolic possibilities of space and movement suggested by the text be explored in rehearsal, until a pattern is established that works for the particular stage and particular actors involved in a production and that is also expressive of the play's inner structure. When Nora looks from her warm living room through the window to the cold world outside, while speaking of her own suicide in the "freezing black water," the play's basic conflict is expressed in a single action. Delivering the speech in this way is thus an example of what Michael Chekhov called the "psychological gesture," an essential movement or bodily attitude that sums up a character and his emotional situation. The psychological gesture "stirs our will power, gives it a definite direction, awakens feelings, and gives us a condensed version of the character."[8]

Here, then, is the nature of Ibsen's theatricality: not just the usual idea of creating lively characters or exciting climaxes, but rather in using the physical realities of the stage, the props and costumes, settings and placements and movements, in structured and expressive ways. We can even place these theatrical elements in a Kierkegaardian scheme similar to the one given already for the characters:

	AESTHETIC	Ironic	ETHICAL
Time	Past	Present (Xmas)	Future
Space	Stove area		Window area
	Living room	Hallways, doors	Outside
	Italy (South)		Norway (North)
Props	Xmas tree (Act 1) ⎯⎯⎯⎯⎯⎯⎯⎯⎯⎯→		Xmas tree (2 and 3)
	gifts, decorations		money
	macaroons		wallet, purse
	cigars		business papers
	tambourine		note (of loan)
	piano		letters
	embroidery		calling cards
Costumes	Tarantella dress		Nora's outdoor clothes
	Masquerade clothes		Muff, gloves, coats,
	Silk stockings		scarfs, etc.
	Men's evening dress		Men's business suits

In this case, of course, the scheme is less precise and complete than the one for the characters. On the one hand, many more items could be added to the lists; on the other, Ibsen does not always spell out *exactly* what he wants in the way of a costume or a piece of business (to do so for the entire play would require a text longer than *War and Peace,* and would still probably be incomplete—if anyone took the trouble to try to follow it and find out), but instead, like any good playwright, he merely suggests *potentialities* for directors, designers, and actors to explore. Thus, all productions of the play will be different—even all *good* productions—but all good productions will in some way be expressive of Ibsen's generating idea.

Francis Fergusson, in his book *The Idea of a Theatre,* has written of the poetic nature of Ibsen's theater:

> It is a hidden poetry, masquerading as reporting; it is a "poetry of the theatre" (in M. Cocteau's phrase) and not a poetry of words; and it is based upon the histrionic sensibility and the art of acting: it can only be seen in performance or by imagining a performance.[9]

Later critics such as John Northam, who come to Ibsen with a thorough knowledge of Norwegian, have perhaps refuted the old notion that there is "not a poetry of words" in Ibsen's drama, but that is not at issue here. Fergusson's main point is still valid: Ibsen is a supreme "poet of the theatre," manipulating the temporal and spatial elements of the stage in the way that a purely verbal poet manipulates words. In *A Doll House,* there is an underlying idea or generative principle—the ethical leap—that informs the elements of plot, characterization, setting, properties, costumes, and movements, despite their externally diverse, realistic qualities. The generative principle is fulfilled only in production, through the actors' performances and (as Fergusson should have added) the realizations of the director and designer as well.

In sum, *A Doll House* can be seen as both mechanistic realism and as a complex poetic structure that employs every aspect of the theater to explore in detail the nature of the leap from Kierkegaard's aesthetic level of life to the ethical level. I shall try to show in the next two chapters that Ibsen's other two social plays are similarly structured, although based in each case on a different unifying principle.

5/The Tragedy of the Aesthetic Life: *Ghosts*

GHOSTS has the best critical reputation of Ibsen's middle plays. Francis Fergusson, G. Wilson Knight, Eric Bentley, Una Ellis-Fermor, and others have written of it with admiration (although it is still widely viewed in the practical theater as a piece of kitchen-sink realism about venereal disease). These critics generally view Mrs. Alving as the tragic heroine of the play, in the traditional, Aristotelian sense. Unfortunately, such a traditional, non-Structuralist view, in which a single character is discussed in isolation, has tended to obscure the articulated web of poetic relationships within the play as a whole. Without ignoring the importance of Mrs. Alving, we should see her characterization only in this context. The play is not just about her, but rather about the aesthetic level of existence. The aesthetic life, as personified in the artist-hero Osvald, is the catalyst for all the events in the play, including the tragic process undergone by Mrs. Alving. It is reflected, as usual, in other characters (including some who are unseen), as well as in theatrical elements like setting and properties. For this reason, I have entitled this chapter "The Tragedy of the Aesthetic Life"—not to supplant Mrs. Alving with Osvald as the central figure, but rather to supplant the very notion of a single, tragic hero by one of an overall, tragic, generative principle.

A Doll House was a tragedy of separation. To embrace the ethical life, as Nora does, is to become like Brand in Ibsen's earlier, Romantic play on the same theme—

separated from spouse and family. The ethical person becomes tough and independent, but also frozen and alone, cut off from warmth, joy, and love. *Ghosts,* on the other hand, is a tragedy of incorporation, of a loss of identity in a formless melting pot like the one the Button Moulder threatens Peer Gynt with. Osvald, artist and child, is a paragon of the aesthetic life, yet he dies young, or rather reverts to a helpless infant because of a ghastly "softening of the brain" brought on by hereditary illness. In contrast to Brand or Nora Helmer, Osvald is reunited with his mother, restored to the bosom of the family in the house where he was born, once again the dependent and loving child like Peer Gynt reunited with Solveig at the end of life's journey, but it is a reunion that leaves him mindless and soulless. As *A Doll House* was concerned with the formation of personality, so *Ghosts* is concerned with the dissolving of personality.

Like *A Doll House, Ghosts* has suffered in the English-speaking world from inept criticism. It was originally valued for the wrong reasons, and then later attacked on the same erroneous grounds, when the Problem Play became devalued in the 1920s. Earning its reputation in England and North America as a tough-minded, serious examination of the Problem (with a capital *P*) of syphilis, *Ghosts* came to be ridiculed as a trivial shocker, whose effect had been totally the result of the sexual hypocrisy of the Victorian age; in the enlightened twentieth century, venereal disease had become a bore. When asked to perform in a revival of the play in the early nineteen-forties, Ethel Barrymore is supposed to have replied, "This is no time for syphilis!" The critical revaluation of Ibsen over the past thirty years has done something to restore the play's literary reputation, but its theatrical reputation remains as low as it was at the time of Barrymore's snide remark; at my own production a few years ago, one reviewer even felt compelled to apologize for having enjoyed what he called "Victorian clap-trap."

Yet there is perhaps more to such attitudes than prejudice. *Ghosts* does appear at first glance to be full of realistic errors—contradictory details, fortuitous events, awkward characterization. The orphanage burns down just as Mrs. Alving is about to reveal the secret of Regina's birth, conveniently delaying the end of the play for another act. The characterization of Manders is a clumsy piece of satire, Ibsen's all-too-obvious attempt to get back at those whom he called "the black band of theologians who rule in Norway," who were inhibiting his son's legal career at the time of the play's composition. It is not clear whether Osvald has a case of congenital syphilis, or picked up a dose on his own, since one minute he says, "I've never lived a wild life—not in any respect" (p. 249), and the next he is saying, "The whole of my life ruined beyond repair—all because of my own carelessness" (p. 251). The latter remark can perhaps be explained by Osvald's confused state when he says it, since he does not yet know the truth about his father, but if the former is true, and his syphilis really is congenital, why does not his mother also have the disease?[2] One does not actually "inherit" syphilis, but receives it directly from the mother's body. And what about Osvald's half-sister, Regina? Impregnated by the ostensibly syphilitic Captain Alving, her mother would have been infected by the disease (we do know that she died young) and have passed it on to her daughter. Yet Regina is repeatedly described in the play as the picture of health, in contrast to her decrepit half-brother.

As with *A Doll House,* however, all these apparent problems disappear if we see Ibsen as a Kierkegaardian Romantic operating through realistic conventions, rather than as a scientific realist writing mechanistic Problem Plays. Consider first the characterization of Manders. We have seen that there is nothing unusual about Ibsen's creating flat, abstract characters; if anything, it is the rule rather than the exception. Manders is merely another ironic character, like Torvald Helmer. There is a worsening of this type through Ibsen's middle period, as his sympathies move more and more toward the aesthetic, represented primarily in this play by Osvald, Manders's antagonist. Torvald Helmer seemed basically decent until his exposure at the end of *A Doll House,* but the audience knows that Manders is a phony within moments of his first appearance, from his feebly disguised sexual interest in Regina:

> MANDERS *(Regarding her).* You know, Miss Engstrand, I definitely think you've grown since I saw you last.
> REGINA. Do you think so, Pastor? Mrs. Alving says that I've filled out, too.
> MANDERS. Filled out—? Well, yes, maybe a little—but acceptably. *(A short pause.)* (P. 210)

His moral weakness is as immediately obvious here as was Engstrand's physical weakness in the previous scene, when Engstrand came in stomping about on a short and twisted leg. But in Ibsen's next play, *An Enemy of the People,* the Mayor is an even worse version of Manders; his hypocrisy is not merely ludicrous but actually destructive.

Since Manders is outwardly ethical, it is with him that the Problem Play material is associated: the debate over the "advanced" books Mrs. Alving has been reading, the debate with Osvald over free love, plus the more general Problem of the venality and shallowness of this typical member of "the black band of theologians." But this is only one aspect of the play, which focuses more and more on Osvald as it progresses, and less and less on Manders. In fact, it appears that Ibsen set out intending to write a Problem Play, but more or less dropped his plan around the middle of the second act, as the characters and their situation began to move with a force of their own. The debates over advanced books and free love in the first act are left open, as if to be resolved later, but the subjects are never again raised. (As Eric Bentley has pointed out, we never even learn the titles of the books!)[3] Manders and Osvald are never onstage together again; instead of building to a climactic confrontation between the two, which we would expect from the first act, the play turns into the tragedy of Osvald. Manders all but disappears from the stage after the middle of Act 2, when he is tricked by Engstrand, although the Pastor has been on almost continuously from the beginning; conversely, Osvald, barely seen up until that point, dominates the stage from the middle to the end. Ibsen's greatest strength as a playwright was always in his endings—usually written very quickly after lengthy and laborious work on the earlier parts—but unfortunately too many people have not looked beyond his beginnings. In this play, the first impression is of a fatuous clergyman, afraid even to get fire insurance for the orphanage from fear that people might interpret it as demonstrating a lack of faith—a heavy and rather cheap satire. But the final scene, which moves in great waves of emotion to the ultimate, awful vision of Osvald regressed to an idiot child as the sun at last burns through the mist and his mother stands paralyzed with terror, recalls the blinded Oedipus or Lear gone mad on the heath.

It is true, then, that the satirization of Manders is a bit extreme. This can be overcome in production, as in my version where the role was cast with an attractive actor who played his part with sincerity rather than for obvious laughs. (After all, Mrs. Alving is supposed to have been in love with him; and, although Manders is a hypocrite, he is totally unaware of his own hypocrisy.) But the important point about Manders's characterization is that it is totally in keeping with the Kierkegaardian scheme; it is part of the play's overall pattern of characterization rather than being simply an independent satirical portrait. Once again, all the characters, including those whom we do not see, can be categorized in Kierkegaardian terms, mirroring and contrasting with one another:

AESTHETIC	Ironic	ETHICAL
	Mrs. Alving (before play) —————(before play)——▶	Mrs. Alving (during play)
Osvald	Manders (unconscious hypocrite; morally deformed)	
Regina	Engstrand (conscious hypocrite; physically deformed)	
Captain Alving (dead)	French doctor (unseen)	
Joanna (dead)		

The first thing noticeable about this scheme in comparison with that of *A Doll House* is the lack of arrows referring to the time of the play's action. This is because *Ghosts*, fundamentally, is not a play of character change, nor even (despite the abundance of "secrets") one of exposure. It is instead a play of *intensification;* as the play proceeds, the characters do not become something different but instead become more and more themselves. Manders in Act 1 is hypocritical, but still on an abstract level; he may leer at Regina but he specifically avoids *doing* anything with her, when she asks if she might come to serve in his house. His discussions of free love, Mrs. Alving's advanced books, the problem of fire insurance, are just that—discussions. But in the last act, he is unwittingly in league with his alter ego,

Engstrand, putting up the money for Engstrand's "Sailor's Home" that we know perfectly well will actually be a brothel.

Similarly, Osvald's madness, which causes him to "revert back to a helpless child again" (p. 272), carries him to the extreme of the aesthetic life, childlike, soulless, dissolved. His insanity is the equivalent of the Button Moulder's melting pot in *Peer Gynt;* and the final scene in which he chants "the sun—the sun" to his horrified mother while the sun rises in the background recalls Peer Gynt in Solveig's arms at the end of that play, a scene that also takes place at sunrise.

Osvald, however, is an upgraded Peer Gynt, with all of Peer's vitality and zest, plus a good deal more intellect and sensitivity. His trip south (to Paris, in this case), his return to his mother, the final scene in which he reverts to a child, are all reminiscent of *Peer Gynt,* but where Peer was merely a clever liar, Osvald is a genuine artist, who has made a name for himself, despite his youth, and who, according to Manders (whom we must certainly believe, since he does not like Osvald), is often mentioned favorably in the newspapers (p. 220). True to his artistic nature, he tends to speak of events in visual terms. He describes Regina as if she were an artist's model: "Isn't she magnificent-looking? The figure she has!" (p. 254). Even his illness he converts into a colorful visual metaphor:

> The doctor said it needn't be fatal at once. He called it a kind of "softening of the brain"—some phrase like that. *(Smiles sadly.)* I think that expression sounds so nice. It always makes me think of cherry-red velvet draperies—something soft to stroke. (P. 273)

Osvald's belief in free love, his smoking and drinking, and his flirtation with Regina are all Gyntish activities, but again, raised to a nobler level. He defends free love and those who practice it in elevated terms, insisting that "in these so-called unconventional homes . . . I've never once heard an offensive word, nor have I ever witnessed anything that could be called immoral" (p. 224); at the same time, he attacks respectable hypocrites (like Manders, we cannot help thinking) who visit Paris and go on sprees:

> OSVALD. But do you know when and where I *have* met immorality among artists?
> MANDERS. No, thank God, I don't!
> OSVALD. Well, then let me tell you. I've met it when one or another of our exemplary husbands and fathers—on a trip away from home and out to see a little life—did the artists the honor of dropping in on them in their poor cafés. Then we had our ears opened wide. Those gentlemen could tell us about things and places we never dreamed existed. (P. 224)

Similarly, Osvald's desire for Regina, while thoroughly unconventional, is not vulgarized, but described with almost religious ecstasy:

> OSVALD. Mother—when I saw her there in front of me, that splendid girl, so alive with health and beauty—it was as if I'd never noticed her before—but now she was standing there as if her arms were simply waiting to take me in—
> MRS. ALVING. Osvald!
> OSVALD. Then it struck me that in her was my salvation, because I saw how the joy of life was in her. (Pp. 255-56)

The phrase *joy of life* (repeated six times in the play), combined with the religious term *salvation,* sums up Osvald's aesthetic philosophy, making it something more than the haphazard insouciance of Peer Gynt, giving it voice and dignity.

But there is another side to the "joy of life," which is shown in Osvald's mental illness, this disease with which he says he is "burning up" (p. 265). As already noted, the details of the disease, which is never named, are quite vague. (Some critics have even gone so far as to suggest that there is no physical illness at all, but that Osvald is a schizophrenic.) Actually, the symptoms fit tuberculosis better than they do syphilis, despite the play's notoriety as a thesis piece about venereal disease. Tuberculosis was believed in Ibsen's time to be hereditary; it also sometimes attacks the brain. Tuberculosis would explain the apparently strange etiology of Osvald's disease—his blaming of it on "carelessness" would not be a euphemism but a literal fact—as well as Mrs. Alving's and Regina's not having it. Furthermore, it would be consistent with Osvald's fever, which is not found in third-stage syphilis. Finally, of course, tuberculosis, or "consumption," was at the time almost the traditional disease of the Romantic artist, as seen in real life no less than in novels, plays, and operas. But before this theory provokes a specious critical controversy, let me disclaim it as a serious point of view. It is interesting only in that it shows how Ibsen was *not* writing a medical tract; Osvald's vague symptoms could probably be associated with any number of diseases. Ibsen was careless with scientific details, as usual, because the disease that Osvald suffers from is not anything to be found in a textbook, but rather is life itself:

> So much that I wanted to do in this world—I don't dare think of it anymore—I'm not *able* to think of it. . . . In a shameful, mindless, trivial way, to have thrown away health, happiness, a world of possibility—my future, my life—! (P. 251)

The poignancy of this speech is not reserved for syphilitics, nor for consumptives or schizophrenics. It has something to say to all of us. To live for the satisfaction of appetite, for drink, art, love, beauty, is to live joyously, but to throw one's life away. One's validity is also one's extinction. The aesthetic characters in the play all die young or burn out early—Captain Alving, Joanna (Regina's mother, the maid whom Captain Alving seduced), Osvald, and probably Regina, who is going to her "ruin" at the end. The tragedy of the aesthetic person is to be melted down, die young, burn out. And yet, like the Phoenix, whose myth informs so much of this play, to burn up in this way is to be reborn: like Peer Gynt, Osvald does not die at the end, but rather reverts to childhood; furthermore, as we are constantly reminded, he is almost the reincarnation of his father. Similarly, Regina reincarnates her mother, Joanna—"If Osvald takes after his father, then I take after my mother, I guess" (p. 268). The burned orphanage will revive as Engstrand's Seamen's Home, bearing Captain Alving's name, as the orphanage did, and even financed by his money (the leftover capital from building the orphanage).

Thus, the tragedy of the aesthetic person is also his validity. Much more than does *Peer Gynt,* whose hero though lovable is found wanting, *Ghosts* glorifies the aesthetic life, in its passion and poignancy. The alternative is to be like Manders, cowardly, inert, unchanging, who insists "I'm the same as I always was" (p. 239). There are actually two kinds of ghosts in the play, those who are continually dying but also continually being reborn, and those like Manders and Mrs. Alving whose lives are dead, frozen and joyless. It is not an easy alternative, but the former kind is shown to be clearly superior; the moral of the play might be summed up in Marvell's famous couplet, "Though we cannot make our sun stand still/Yet we will make him run."

The third of the major characters, Mrs. Alving, is the only character in the play at the ethical level. This was not so before the play began—her marriage to Captain Alving, for example, was a hypocritical farce. There were no depths to which she would not sink in order to keep up a respectable name for herself and her husband:

> I've endured a lot in this house to keep him home in the evenings—and nights, I had to become his drinking companion as he got sodden over his bottle, holed up in his room. There I had to sit alone with him, forcing myself through his jokes and toasts and all his maundering, abusive talk, and then fight him bare-handed to drag him into bed—(P. 230)

Here was the "ironic" life at its worst; both the ethical *and* the aesthetic aspects were a sham, as she kept up a respectable façade for the public and a convivial one for her husband. The scheme for creating an orphan's home in her husband's name was similarly in a hypocritical vein. It is interesting that in this play, which is so concerned with children, we never actually see any of the orphans who are to benefit from her project, nor hear one mentioned by name. The orphans were to be merely the pawns of Mrs. Alving, a means to her end of maintaining respectability: "The orphanage was meant to spike all the rumors and dispell the doubts" (p. 230). After the orphanage has burned to the ground, she recognizes that "it's best that it went like this. This orphanage was never made for anyone's benefit" (p. 262).

It is ironic that Mrs. Alving would choose to endow an orphanage, and not, say, a hospital or a public library; again, Ibsen maintains symbolic control over realistic detail. The pattern is always that Mrs. Alving damaged her children—Osvald, her actual son, as well as the surrogates, Regina and the orphans. The damage was always in spite of her good intentions, because the goodness of those intentions was rooted in a fear of shame rather than genuine love. Her cover-up of her husband's aesthetic nature and her endowing of the orphanage were phony, the kind of thing that an "ironic" character like Manders would do, and it is significant that Manders had a hand in both actions: when at one point she actually did run away from her husband, and offered herself to Manders in what would have been one of the very "free love" liaisons that Manders finds so shocking, he sent her away, back to her "duty" and her husband (pp. 225-26). She then had no choice but to pursue the hypocritical strategy with regard to her husband that is described above. Now, at the beginning of the play, she is working with Manders in setting up the orphanage, and once again the focus is on propriety, in this case on the fire insurance that Manders, hilariously, fears would be taken by the populace as evidence that neither he nor Mrs. Alving had "adequate faith in Divine Providence" (p. 216).

Nevertheless, by the time the play begins, Mrs. Alving has really left this "ironic" level. Her ethical leap has already taken place; she has been reading books with advanced views, and she repeatedly challenges Manders's stodgy ideas. She supports Osvald in the debate on free love, and, most important, ends the cover-up about her husband by telling Manders flat out what her marriage was actually like. In the second act she denounces Manders for having sent her away those many years ago, calling it "a crime against us both" (p. 239), and when the orphanage burns down, her thoughts are not of the lack of insurance, as are Manders's, but rather of the fitting nature of the fire's destroying an orphanage that was a sham. And finally, she confesses to Osvald and Regina the facts of her marriage, recognizing that the moral fault was hers, not her husband's. But she did not need the fire to stimulate her to do this; in fact, she had been about to make the same confession just as the fire broke out. Her level of moral development is such that she would probably have revealed the truth about her husband to the whole world, fire or no fire. No doubt following the ideas in her "advanced books," she feels a compulsion to clear the air, to confess, to be honest for the first time in decades. True to her ethical nature, Mrs. Alving takes the blame for her disastrous marriage on herself: "I made this home unbearable for your poor father" (p. 267). She recognizes that there is more to morality than respectability, that ethics is not a matter of merely doing what is generally conceded to be correct, but rather an inner compulsion, an inner devotion to truth and decency, which often conflicts with what is popularly considered to be ethical.

The pattern, again, is that she, like Manders and Osvald, has been becoming more and more her true self. The abstract questions of morality, represented by the advanced books in Act 1, have become actual moral *acts* on her part, exposing the truth to Manders, then to Osvald and Regina, and finally exposing the ultimate truth about herself to herself. *She* caused the bad marriage; it was not her husband's fault for not living up to moral standards, since he had no moral sense at all, but her own fault for not being sensitive and honest. But the extreme for Mrs. Alving does not come until the very end of the play. In being forced to consider the killing of her own child, she faces the same dilemma as Abraham with Isaac, the subject of Kierkegaard's *Fear and Trembling*. Now neither morality in the popular sense nor her own developed sense of inner morality can be of any use to her. People often asked Ibsen whether she actually will give Osvald the morphine pills; Ibsen always answered ambiguously, because the point is that the dilemma *is* morally ambiguous. As with Abraham, it would be immoral to kill her son, but it would also be immoral *not* to kill him. In her case, of course, it is not God who is commanding the killing, but her son himself, who did not want to live on for years as a mindless invalid. To kill him would release him from this horror, but it would also be murder, and murder of the person nearest and dearest to her in the world. Back in the first act the ethical life, as represented in her advanced books, appeared to her to be a fairly easy thing that made her "feel more secure" (p. 213). The books did not even seem to be anything very special:

> There's actually nothing really new in these books, nothing beyond what most people think and believe. It's simply that most people don't like to face these things, or what they imply. (P. 213)

With each successive revelation, however, Mrs. Alving has learned that an ethical devotion is *not* so easy as the books perhaps implied, and in the final moment the books are no good at all. The agony of Mrs. Alving's plight demonstrates the tragedy of the ethical life: it is that there are at times no moral "universals," but only moral *contexts,* and different contexts can imply opposing moral imperatives. Such imperatives are not "categorical," as Kant insisted, but only relative. The ethical life has led Mrs. Alving to a brutal but logical conclusion. "Thou shalt not kill" exists co-equally with "Thou shalt kill."

In *Ghosts* we thus see a trio of major characters representing Kierkegaard's aesthetic, ironic, and ethical levels of existence. It is a play of extremes, which may explain Ibsen's heavy treatment of Manders—being invalid from the start, his characterization in becoming extreme becomes perhaps overly satirical. But we should note that the other two major characters are taken to extremes as well.

There is not much good that can be said about the ironic level, represented by Manders, and there is a great deal to be said for the aesthetic and ethical represented by Osvald and Mrs. Alving; yet both aesthetic and ethical are shown in the end to be lacking. As in Kierkegaard, they are valid levels of existence, but ultimately they have limitations, leading man to paradoxes that cannot be resolved within the standards of the level itself. Osvald's life is joyous, yet in the end, mindless and soulless; Mrs. Alving's life is now ethical, but it leads her in the end to an impossible moral dilemma. No one escapes his level in *Ghosts,* but instead follows its implications to their tragic ultimate.

As in *A Doll House,* Ibsen's treatment here of the lesser characters and of the details of staging are consistent with his Kierkegaardian scheme. Ibsen again employs the Shakespearean device of having minor characters reflect the major ones. As already noted, Regina, Captain Alving, and Joanna all reflect the principal character, Osvald, and establish the reincarnation theme, with the two younger characters, Osvald and Regina, "taking after" their parents, Captain Alving and Joanna. Osvald and Regina not only start to repeat their parents' amorous activities, causing Mrs. Alving to call them "ghosts" at the end of Act 1; they also reflect their parents' aesthetic attributes generally, and reflect one another. Regina, for example, is learning French and wants to go to Paris just as Osvald did. She flirts with Manders as well as with Osvald, expresses an interest in clothes (pp. 207-8), in champagne (pp. 256, 269), in Manders's money (p. 268). In the end she decides that she may go to her father's new brothel, an act to which Mrs. Alving, true to her ethical nature, reacts with horror:

> REGINA. And if things really go wrong, I still know a house where I'll do just fine.
> MRS. ALVING. Where?
> REGINA. In "Captain Alving's Home."
> MRS. ALVING. Regina—I can see now—you'll go to your ruin! (P. 269)

Regina, however, reacts to Mrs. Alving with characteristically unself-conscious amorality:

REGINA. Ahh, ffft! *Adieu. (She curtsies and goes out the hall door.)* (P. 269)

Regina had been obviously attracted to Osvald, yet when she learned that he was ill she threw him over as casually as she would have discarded a worn-out dress, saying cold-bloodedly, "I really can't stay out in the country and run myself ragged for invalids" (p. 268). She brings to mind the maid Anne-Marie in *A Doll House,* who readily left her own daughter with strangers in order to become little Nora's nurse, or Peer Gynt, who forgot his mother after she died. Regina is capable of genuine feeling, but only of a direct and selfish kind. As soon as her love encounters an obstacle, it evaporates.

Of Joanna, Regina's mother, we know very little except her actions: she was a maid in the Alving's house, became pregnant by Captain Alving, was kicked out of the house but given some money, more or less paid Engstrand to marry her, lied and said her seducer had been a foreigner on a yacht (even Engstrand does not know the truth about Regina's parentage), and died soon after. All these are Gyntish, aesthetic actions; in addition, Ibsen gives Joanna a characteristic, ungrammatical little phrase, "Leave me be," which we hear repeated from two independent sources, Engstrand (p. 205), and Mrs. Alving (p. 229). Thus this minor character, long gone from the scene, is brought to life; Joanna's "ghost" walks the stage.

The characterization of Captain Alving is even better developed. We learn of his amorous activities, his drinking and carousing, and his smoking; in addition, in the passage already quoted, we learn of his relationship with his wife:

MRS. ALVING. I've endured a lot in this house to keep him home in the evenings—and nights, I had to become his drinking companion as he got sodden over his bottle, holed up in his room. There I had to sit alone with him, forcing myself through his jokes and toasts and all his maundering, abusive talk, and then fight him barehanded to drag him into bed—(P. 230)

The focus at this point is on Mrs. Alving and what she "endured," but it is interesting to consider the relationship from her husband's point of view. How odd that he would put up with such an arrangement, which apparently went on for years, without being tempted to go back to his cronies in the taverns and brothels! Ibsen's aesthetic characters tend to be surprisingly devoted to their families, and highly capable of love—of a sort. Even Regina, we feel, would have become a good wife for Osvald, if it had not been for his illness. Mrs. Alving, of course, was incapable of appreciating her husband's loving nature at that time; only at the end of the play does she recognize his inherent goodness:

> MRS. ALVING. You should have known your father when he was just a young lieutenant. *He* had the joy of life, he did!
> OSVALD. Yes, I know.
> MRS. ALVING. It was like a holiday just to look at him. And all the energy, the unquenchable power that was in him!
> OSVALD. Well—?
> MRS. ALVING. And then, so full of that very joy, this child—because he *was* like a child then, really—had to make a life here in a mediocre town that had no joys to offer—only distractions.... Your poor father never found any outlet for the overpowering joy of life that he had. And I'm afraid I couldn't make his home very festive, either. (Pp. 266-67)

It is interesting that the key metaphor she chooses at this point to describe him is a family one—"this child." This of course foreshadows Osvald's reverting to helpless childhood shortly after this speech, and adds to the "children" motif already established through the orphanage, Osvald, and Regina. Mrs. Alving was once again guilty of inadvertent *Kindermord*. But the metaphor also establishes a tone of familial coziness to the aesthetic life, which is the source of both its charm and, as we see at the end of the play, its tragedy.

Engstrand, as a hypocritical character, reflects Manders. As with Manders, his "ironic" nature is strongly delineated. John Northam points out that Engstrand "uses two languages":

> His first is a coarser version of Regine's: "out on a binge," "half-seas over," "what the hell" are characteristic. His second, high-lighted by being jammed into close juxtaposition with his first, is larded, not with directly social clichés as Regine's is, but with clichés of a moral or religious kind. "I was out on a binge last night. Yes, for we humans are weak, my child"; and ". . . when I was half-seas over. . . . Temptations are manifold in this world" are sequences of this sort. There are other clichés: "God's own rain," "a father's guiding hand," "what a child owes its father," etc.
>
> This interplay of languages serves first of all, and obviously, to characterize Engstrand as a gross hypocrite; indeed by the time he leaves the stage his crippled leg is likely to have established itself as a visual image of his undoubted moral depravity.[4]

The equating of the crippled leg with Engstrand's hypocrisy is made more explicit in Act 2; we know perfectly well that he received the injury in some kind of drunken tavern brawl, but he has actually managed to convince Manders, who as usual sees only surfaces, that he received it as a result of religious devotion!

> ENGSTRAND. Yes, you remember, Pastor, how I once took it on myself to go into a dance hall where common

seamen were rioting in drink and dissipation, like they say. And when I tried to arouse them to seek out a better life—
MRS. ALVING *(over by the window).* Hm—
MANDERS. Yes, I know, Engstrand; those ruffians threw you downstairs. You've told me that before. Your disability does you great credit. (P. 243)

For Manders, the leg is a sign of Engstrand's moral rectitude; for the audience, a sign of his moral depravity. The leg is thus a powerful "ironic" symbol. Yet despite this strong visual image and the meanings associated with it, Engstrand is a far more attractive character than Manders. If Regina, Joanna, and Captain Alving are somewhat downgraded versions of the artist Osvald, Engstrand is a somewhat upgraded version of the phony Manders. This is because Engstrand's hypocrisy is at least conscious, while Manders, to the very end, is unaware of the flaws in his own character. Throughout most of the play there is an unequal battle going on between Engstrand and his alter ego. Engstrand always wins out over the foolish Pastor because of Engstrand's combination of Gyntish lying and a shrewd sense of the predictability of his opponent's morality. Their major confrontation occurs in Act 2, in the scene from which the above quotation is taken; Manders has called in Engstrand in order to confront him with the truth about Regina's paternity. He is furious with Engstrand for having lied to him, but Engstrand quickly manipulates Manders with pious phrases. Engstrand lied to protect Joanna's and the child's reputation, it seems, and the money she brought was put entirely into the upbringing of the child. Manders is cowed, and agrees to a devotional service at the new orphanage, which leads to his final undoing at Engstrand's hands. Engstrand burns down the orphanage and makes the Pastor think that he, Manders, started the blaze, thus putting Manders eternally in Engstrand's power, and specifically getting the money left over from the orphanage and the sale of the land for a mortgage for Engstrand's "Sailor's Home." Engstrand's ability to think quickly and manipulate Manders can be astounding:

> ENGSTRAND. And I saw so plainly how the pastor took that candle and pinched it out with his fingers and flicked the tip of the wick down into those shavings.
> MANDERS. You saw me do that?
> ENGSTRAND. Plain as day, I saw it.
> MANDERS. I just don't understand it. It's never been a habit of mine to snuff a candle in my fingers.
> ENGSTRAND. Yes, it did look pretty sloppy to me, all right. (P. 261)

Instantly Engstrand turns Manders's attempted excuse into additional accusation! The vigor displayed by Engstrand suggests new possibilities for the ironic life, which Ibsen was to explore further in his next play, *An Enemy of the People;* never before had an "ironic" character in an Ibsen play been given any validity at all, but Engstrand's shrewdness and verbal agility give him a certain authenticity.

He is capable of deceiving himself, however. The most hilarious line in the play comes near the end when Engstrand has received a promise of the money for "Captain Alving's Home" for sailors. Engstrand says piously to Mrs. Alving, "I think I can promise you it'll be truly worthy of that great man's memory" (p. 264). In the production that I directed, this line never failed to get a huge laugh, which is a tribute to Ibsen's skill, since the irony is so complex: Engstrand, sharing the widespread view of Captain Alving's fine reputation, thinks he is putting one over on Mrs. Alving. Manders, who knows of the Captain's true nature, is made uneasy, but does not realize that the home will actually be a brothel. Mrs. Alving and the audience, however, know of both Captain Alving's true self *and* the truth about the sailor's home, which truly *will* be worthy of him.

There is one additional character mentioned in the play, the French doctor whom Osvald saw in Paris when the symptoms of the disease were first upon him. There is a doctor in almost every one of Ibsen's plays, a fact that makes this one worth looking at even though he is mentioned very briefly. Osvald says that "he was one of the foremost doctors down there" (p. 250), and quotes him twice. "Right from your birth, your whole system has been more or less worm-eaten," the doctor told him, and then, "that old cynic said, 'the sins of the fathers are visited upon the children'" (p. 250). The stressing of the doctor's eminence ("one of the foremost") echoes Manders's obsession with reputation; furthermore, the moralistic tone, in a downgraded biblical reference coming from an "old cynic," shows that this doctor, at least in Osvald's eyes, was a hypocrite. From this short description we get, once again, the reflection of one of the major characters. The doctor is at the ironic level, again foreshadowing Ibsen's next play, in which a doctor of the ironic type is the hero. Even in this very minor (and unseen) character, then, Ibsen's artistic control is complete. Always he channels the play's realistic material into clear, powerful structures, so that every detail of the apparent "slice of life" helps to convey his allegorical meaning.

The setting, like the characters, also shows this controlled significance. The onstage setting in *A Doll House* was, as we saw, an emblem for the aesthetic life; it was Nora's refuge, a cozy nest insulating her from the cold realities of the outer world. The room in which *Ghosts* takes place is different, with its large greenhouse at the back through which the rain, mist, and fjord landscape can be seen. Osvald would *like* it to be a refuge; in Act 2 he speaks of his joy in returning home in escapist terms:

I think it's so cozy, Mother. *(Patting and fondling her.)* Imagine—what it is for me, coming home, to sit at my mother's own table, in my mother's room, and enjoy her delectable meals. (P. 247)

But immediately he becomes restless and upset:

OSVALD *(somewhat impatiently, walking about and smoking).* And what else am I going to do here? I can't accomplish anything—
MRS. ALVING. Can't you?
OSVALD. In all this murk? Not a glimmer of sunlight the whole day long? (P. 247)

In performance, of course, the "murk" is fully visible. In our production, Osvald walked up to the greenhouse at this point, so that he was actually looking out at the mist as he spoke of it. Furthermore, the rain is continuing to fall during this scene, creating both a visual and audible presence behind it, a constant background of gloom. In *A Doll House* there was a single window to the outside that occasionally cast reminders of the cold reality lurking there; in this play, the outside is a force that has invaded and completely conquered the room. As John Northam has pointed out, this pattern of invasion is established in the opening moments of the play, when Regina is trying to keep Engstrand out of the room because he is soaking wet.[5] She fails, and he enters soggy and dripping into the living room. It is significant that, unlike *A Doll House,* there is no mention in the stage directions or the dialogue of any stove. The chill, damp world of the outside seems at one with the room; Mrs. Alving, long ago, filled the house with such obligations of "duty" that it snuffed out all remnants of joy and warmth:

They'd drilled me so much in duty and things of that kind that I went on here all too long putting my faith in them. Everything resolved into duties—*my* duties, and *his* duties, and—I'm afraid I made this home unbearable for your poor father. (P. 267)

In the person of Mrs. Alving, the ethical life "invaded" the house and stifled Captain Alving, as it now threatens to stifle Osvald, until at the very end of the play there is another kind of invasion into the room, as the sun's rays burn through the mist and pour through the huge windows. Simultaneously, Osvald idiotically chants "the sun—the sun" (p. 276); the warmth and light he craved has at last broken through, burning out his brain as well as burning off the actual fog outside.

This characterization of the room has important implications for the stage designer. Because of the title of the play, the setting has often been given a dark, gothic quality, as if the designer were creating the decor for a Hollywood horror film. This is definitely *not* the kind of ghostliness that Ibsen wanted. If his stage directions are followed, the setting will seem not dark but gray, because of the large, dominant greenhouse windows. In the production that I directed, we loaded the greenhouse with as many plants as we could afford, to add to the feeling of dampness and the impression of the outside making an intrusion on the room. The room itself was sparsely furnished, and it had a gray wallpaper almost the same color as the mist itself. The few warm elements in the play, such as the lamp Regina brings on, or Captain Alving's pipe, seemed to be swallowed by the foggy grayness. The house stands for the ethical life at its most stifling.

There are actually three houses mentioned in the play, all oddly enough named after Captain Alving: the family home itself, the orphanage, and the "Sailors' Home." All are in a sense "ironic" emblems, contrasting the good name of Captain Alving with the reality of his life. At the time of the play, however, Captain Alving is long dead, and the family home completely given over to the ethical; it is really *Mrs.* Alving's home. The hypocrisy about her husband's reputation has been shifted over to the orphanage, the most "ironic" of the three homes. The "Sailors' Home" is the least respectable of them all; while the orphanage, if it had not burned down, at least had an ethical purpose, it is obvious that the sailors' home will have no charitable function at all. As a brothel, it will be "truly worthy of that great man's memory," requiring no fire to establish poetic justice; it is already the perfect monument to the man. Thus the trio of houses can be seen as itself reflecting the three Kierkegaardian categories operating under the play, as schematized below along with the other scenic elements:

AESTHETIC	*Ironic*	ETHICAL
Sailors' Home	Orphanage	Family Home
Sun, warmth, light		fog, cold, darkness
France		Norway
lamp		advanced books
pipe		business papers
champagne		money
hot chocolate		greenhouse
food		
liqueur		
cigar		

If the houses are a triad, the other background elements are strongly bipolar. The contrast between light and darkness, sun and mist, is most striking. As already noted, Manders is strongly associated with mist and darkness, a connection that is reinforced by his costuming. Actually, the play's stage directions do not describe his attire, but if he wears the typical clerical garb of the period, he, like Brand, will appear in black. (Remember that Ibsen himself had referred to "the black band of theologians" in describing his inspiration for writing *Ghosts.*) The sight of this black figure on his initial entrance, carrying a black umbrella, drifting in through the misty garden and entering the greenhouse (the same entrance that Engstrand has just used), establishes him in the audience's mind as a dark, foggy, stifled individual.

Set against this is the audience's visual impression of Osvald. The stage directions mention nothing about this but his "wearing a light overcoat, hat in hand" (p. 219), but again, if he is given the typical Parisian artist's attire of the nineteenth century, it will appear light, colorful, and dashing in comparison with the stiff blackness of Manders. (Stanislavski, in his production at the Moscow Art Theatre, made Osvald's undescribed "hat" a beret, an excellent choice.) Osvald's paintings, he says, are filled "with light and sun and holiday scenes—and faces radiant with human content" (p. 257), and the choice of the "radiant" *(strålende)* metaphor is not accidental. There are over thirty references to light or heat in the play, ranging from the barely noticeable, like the hot chocolate that Osvald drinks in Act 1; to the spectacular, like the orphanage fire; to the terrifying, like Osvald's chant, "the sun—the sun," as the sun's rays break through at the end. The references are associated with the aesthetic characters—Captain Alving and his pipe; Regina "blushing all shades of red" (p. 255), who carries a lamp (p. 252); Osvald's cigar. Engstrand's matches might be said to be associated with his hidden, aesthetic side; and, of course, Osvald says of his disease that he is "burning up" (p. 265). As already discussed in chapter 2, heat and light in the play are ambiguous symbols, embodying the reincarnation theme, simultaneously the force of life and the force of destruction.

Conversely, the images of fog and cold, and the dank greenhouse (which might be better described by its British name, "conservatory"), stand for quiescence, inertia, and gloom.

The North-South polarity, which was so strong in the earlier plays, is repeated in *Ghosts,* with Italy replaced by Paris. Osvald contrasts life in Paris with that in Norway in the same kind of terms that Ibsen himself applied to his own initial impressions of Italy:

> OSVALD. I mean, here everyone's brought up to believe that work is a curse and a punishment, and that life is a miserable thing that we're best advised to be out of as soon as possible.
> MRS. ALVING. A vale of tears, yes. And we ingeniously manage to make it that.
> OSVALD. But they won't hear of such things down there. Nobody abroad believes in that sort of outlook anymore. Down there, simply to be alive in the world is held for a kind of miraculous bliss. (P. 257)

It is significant that Osvald repeatedly refers to Paris as "down there," repeating the up-down motif of the earlier plays in contrasting the ethical and aesthetic levels. Ibsen is once again the consummate "poet of the theater," manipulating both visual and verbal elements of the stage in order to create a clear and sustained image. Even the most minor details, such as casual metaphors or briefly handled props, add to this image, which provides a thoroughgoing depiction of the polarized ethical and aesthetic levels, as well as the intermediate ironic level. The realistic façade, the "slice of life," is an illusion; behind it is a Romantic tragedy of character, in which character is fate, driving each individual to its cruel extreme.

To sum up, where *A Doll House* was a realistic reworking of the material in *Brand,* so *Ghosts* is a realistic reworking of the material in *Peer Gynt.* As with *Peer Gynt,* the tragic content of *Ghosts* is set in a strangely comic frame, embodying rhythms of incorporation, reunion, and regeneration. But *Ghosts* is ultimately more tragic than either *Peer Gynt* or *A Doll House;* it lacks the gaiety of the former, and the element of choice in the latter. The characters either have no choice, like Osvald, or an impossible choice, like Mrs. Alving. It is a Gordian knot, which Ibsen will try to unravel with his next play.

6/The Validity of the Ironic Life: *An Enemy of the People*

THE ending of *Ghosts* presents us with a dilemma: both the aesthetic and the ethical life seem to bring man to a dead end, an agonizing yet logical conclusion from which there is no escape. A strictly Kierkegaardian solution would consist of a leap to the religious level, a possibility that Ibsen explores in his late plays, particularly *The Wild Duck*. But first, in *An Enemy of the People*, Ibsen explores another possibility, that the intermediate level between the aesthetic and the ethical, the ironic, might actually have validity. This not only contradicts Kierkegaard's beliefs, it contradicts all of Ibsen's earlier plays, in which the ironic characters are generally shown as hypocrites or phonies, like Helmer in *A Doll House* or Manders in *Ghosts*. This is the basic reason why *Enemy* has always seemed anomalous, not truly a full-fledged member of the Ibsen canon. Yet, although the play is in strict terms non-Kierkegaardian, it retains and even fulfills Kierkegaard's threefold aesthetic-ethical-ironic pattern. *An Enemy of the People* is actually a culmination of the trilogy of social plays, both resolving the problems (and I do not mean just the social ones) of the earlier ethical and aesthetic plays, and opening the way for the "religious" plays to come.

Critics have not recognized this culminating position of *An Enemy of the People*. Its reputation is low—the lowest, not only among the three social plays, but perhaps the lowest of all of Ibsen's works—and it is rarely performed.[1]

Modern critical studies of Ibsen usually skip over *Enemy* entirely, or dismiss it with a few brief phrases, as when John Northam, one of the finest of contemporary Ibsen critics, writes, "it is the least imaginative of all Ibsen's realistic prose dramas; it was written in the shortest time; it contains the fewest examples of visual suggestion."[2] These are typical disparagements. But only the second can be taken as literally true, and even it can be attacked on the ground that Ibsen always wrote very fast once he had solved the basic problems of plot and character in his plays. (*Peer Gynt,* twice as long as *Enemy,* was written almost as quickly.) These solutions probably occurred sooner than usual in the case of *Enemy* because, as we shall see, much of its plotting and characterization were directly based on an earlier play. As for Northam's other complaints, I hope to show that they are decidedly wrong.

The basic problem with *Enemy* comes down to deciding just how seriously we are supposed to take the central character, Dr. Stockmann. Early critics and performers seem to have taken him very seriously. Audiences at Stanislavski's 1905 production even stormed the stage to shake the hand of Stanislavski, playing Dr. Stockmann as a noble hero. The fact that Stockmann is on the side of truth and opposed by a repressive town government was enough, during the 1905 revolution, to make liberal Russians identify with him; the facts that he is opposed by the townspeople as well, and that he makes strongly *anti*democratic speeches to them in Act 4, were ignored in the heat of the moment. But later, in less revolutionary times, and when Ibsen's reputation as a political radical had faded, some critics came to a different view. John Gassner, for example, noting ironies in Dr. Stockmann's characterization, viewed the play as a kind of dark comedy:

> *An Enemy of the People* is intrinsically a comedy.... Before the curtain falls the good doctor has seen his

supporters desert him when he tried to have the baths condemned; and he has made a fool of himself in trusting the careerists and householders of the towns. But he has given them an enormous piece of his truly ponderous mind, and he will continue his defiance. Moreover, he is going to take ragamuffins off the street and try to turn them into idealists by educating them in his home. Stockmann is assuredly Don Quixote in a frock-coat![3]

But Gassner's was a minority viewpoint. The solid majority still hold to the original, noble-hero-against-reaction picture of Dr. Stockmann—except that this is now seen as a flaw rather than a virtue. Eric Bentley specifically rejects Gassner's representation of the Doctor:

> Are you going to say that Stockmann is not Ibsen? There is precious little evidence within the play that the latter is critical of his creation. The whole play breathes the perennial self-complacency of the arrogant idealist. . . . That Ibsen felt compelled to show the other side of the medal in *The Wild Duck* can hardly comfort the critic of *An Enemy of the People*. It takes more than two one-sided plays to make a single two-sided masterpiece. And *An Enemy* is one-sided, a play of moral blacks and whites. To read it as a subtle study in self-righteousness, like *Le Misanthrope*, would be to conceive another play. Stockmann is an Alceste taken pretty much at his own valuation.[4]

Bentley is right is seeing that Gassner went too far in pushing his comic view of Stockmann. Gassner was overlooking the *tone* of the play, which is hardly wry or witty, but rather is blunt and straightforward. If there are ambiguities in the characterization of Dr. Stockmann (and I agree with Gassner that there are), there are none in those of the other characters. "Dark comedies" usually spread their "darkness" throughout the whole work, so that secondary characters like Sancho Panza in *Don Quixote* or

Célimène in *Le Misanthrope* are as ambiguous in their own ways as are the principal characters in theirs, but in *Enemy*, the Mayor, the townspeople, Captain Horster, Petra, and so on, are all distinct and predictable character types of the sort we have seen in Ibsen's earlier plays. But more important, nothing in the character of Dr. Stockmann contradicts the truth of what he says. He is not tilting at windmills; the baths *are* polluted and the majority *are* wrong. These are indeed "moral blacks and whites."

Nevertheless, Bentley also overstates his case. Dr. Stockmann *is* self-righteous, whether a "subtle study" or not. Only a naive audience (such as Stanislavski's) would take "pretty much at his own valuation" a character who makes statements like the following:

> I'll smash them into the ground and shatter them! I'll wreck their defenses in the eyes of every fair-minded man! That's what I'll do! . . . All these lunkheads in the old generation have to be dumped. And that means: no matter *who* they are! I've had such endless vistas opening up for me today. I haven't quite clarified it yet, but I'm working it out. (Pp. 327-28)

Spiteful, rambling, overwrought speeches like these are hardly those of a high-minded scientist in search of the truth. This vague tirade sounds instead like King Lear's blithering diatribe against his daughters: "I will have such revenges on you both/That all the world shall—I will do such things—/What they are yet I know not . . ." (2.4. 278-80). And like Lear, Dr. Stockmann again and again shows boundless egotism, his favorite pronoun being the first person singular:

> If it had been only a few days ago that anyone had tried to gag me like this tonight—I'd have fought for my sacred human rights like a lion! But it doesn't matter to me now. Because now I have greater things to discuss.

I've been thinking a lot these past few days—pondering so many things that finally my thoughts began running wild— .... But then I got everything in place again, and I saw the whole structure so distinctly. It's why I'm here this evening. I have great disclosures to make, my friends. I'm going to unveil a discovery to you. (P. 352)

"Me ... I ... me ... I ... "; we wonder when he will ever stop talking about himself and come to the point!

Dr. Stockman's attitudes and behavior, like his speeches, are also often questionable. Right from the beginning, he is *happy* that the baths are polluted, though it can hardly do either him or the town any good in the long run. Like his brother the Mayor, we cannot help wondering why the good Doctor refused to go through ordinary channels in making his investigations—why he insisted from the first on working behind people's backs. The excuses he gives are lame, like, "Maybe I should have run out in the streets, blabbering about it before I had sure proof. No thanks, I'm not that crazy" (p. 299). Dr. Stockmann's very name describes his ironic character: like Brand, his name means stick ("stokk," in Norwegian), and he can be considered as a rod of chastisement; but the word "stokk" is often also used idiomatically in Norwegian to describe something, or someone, stiff and unyielding. Dr. Stockmann is an instrument of castigation against the Mayor and the townspeople, who are indeed in the wrong, but he is also stubborn and inflexible, taking an "all or nothing" attitude without the slightest attempt to understand their point of view, and clearly enjoying his martyrdom. In fact, he twice compares himself to Christ, once in the crowd scene in Act 4, when he says, "I'm not as meek as one certain person: I'm not saying, 'I forgive them, because they know not what they do'" (pp. 364-65), and again at the end of the play when he calls for disciples—"at least twelve boys to begin with" (p. 385). Dr. Stockmann may be right and his opponents reprehensible, but he has a rather grand and exaggerated way of seeing himself in relation to a small-town political squabble. Brand, another small-town leader, specifically refused to be compared to Christ when Gerd, the mountain girl, tried to make the association, insisting instead that he was "the meanest thing that crawls on earth"; Stockmann, a far less noble figure than Brand, finds the comparison delightful.

In the final tableau of the play, Ibsen has set up a visual irony that is not always noticeable to readers, but which again exposes Dr. Stockmann's inaccurate and exaggerated vision of himself. Alan Reynolds Thompson has shrewdly pointed this out:

> No doubt you recall Dr. Stockman's curtain line, that "the strongest man in the world is he who stands most alone." Most of the critics who quote that line have failed to notice the tableau that Ibsen arranged for the audience to see as the curtain falls on *An Enemy of the People*. There is the good doctor in the middle, with his wife on one side of him and his daughter on the other. That tableau is Ibsen's quiet joke at the expense of his hero.[5]

Thompson might have added that, in addition to Mrs. Stockmann and Petra, Dr. Stockmann's two sons, plus his friend Captain Horster, are gathered around him as well. Though a hero, Stockmann retains the support and comfort of his family, and, as we have seen, a connection with family is a decidedly "aesthetic" trait for Ibsen's characters. Dr. Stockmann is both a Brand (who ended up really standing alone) and a Peer Gynt, with more than just a Solveig to support him at the end.

There is considerable evidence in the play, then, that even though Dr. Stockmann is on the side of truth and progress, his motives are not pure. It was common for

Ibsen to give a character an ambiguous relation to issues that are themselves morally certain in an abstract sense: Gregers Werle in *The Wild Duck* is an obvious example, but others include Brand's harassment of the selfish villagers (a pattern repeated in *Enemy*), or Mrs. Alving's coldness toward her dissolute husband in *Ghosts*. We would perhaps understand the paradox of Dr. Stockmann's position better by recognizing that, just as *A Doll House* was to a certain extent a rewrite of *Brand* and *Ghosts* a rewrite of *Peer Gynt*, so too is *An Enemy of the People* a rewrite of an earlier work—the satirical play *The League of Youth* (1869). Both plays deal with small-town politics and prejudice. The important character of Aslaksen, the cowardly printer, appears in both plays; in *Enemy* he actually refers at one point to a man with the same name as the hero of *The League of Youth:*

> ASLAKEN. In that editor's chair, right there, your predecessor, Councilman Stensgaard, used to sit.
> BILLING *(spits)*. Pah! That renegade.
> HOVSTAD. I'm no double-dealer—and I never will be. (P. 329)

"Double-dealer" describes Stensgaard accurately: he is an utterly amoral young politician with a marvelous gift for public speaking, who with an impulsive speech forms the "League of Youth" to combat the vested interests in the town, and then almost as quickly sells out to those same interests when it suits his career. He has been described as "a political Peer Gynt," but his speeches also foreshadow Dr. Stockmann's:

> They want to deny you the right to speak! You heard them. They want to muzzle you! Away with such tyranny! I don't want to stand here making speeches to a lot of gagged creatures. I'm going to make myself heard!

And you are going to make yourselves heard, too. And we'll say exactly what we like!⁶

The difference is that Stensgaard has no real issue, no polluted baths, to make his cause genuine; and, far from becoming "An Enemy of the People," he always has them in the palm of his hand.

The satire in *The League of Youth* is too heavy. Politicians are self-seeking and their followers are venal; the moral is cheap even if it is valid. Stensgaard has few redeeming qualities, and his techniques are obvious—no audience member could ever imagine himself being taken in by him. In *An Enemy of the People* the heavy political satire is shifted to lesser characters, particularly the treacherous newspapermen. The hero, Dr. Stockmann, is more complex than Stensgaard, his situation more desperate, and the satire more subtle—so subtle, alas, that it has often been missed. Stockmann is not a politician but a doctor. Although he is as vain and self-seeking as Stensgaard, he has a genuine cause with which to advance himself. The baths' pollution is presented in the play not as a vague, emotional issue like the "vested interests" in *The League of Youth* but as an objective fact. Ibsen carefully arranges that this information comes from outside the world of the play, via a letter from a chemist at a university, neither of which is named, nor ever mentioned again after the first act. For the audience, the scientific truth of the polluted water is thus never at issue; instead, the play's focus is on the various characters' *reactions* to this unquestionable fact.

I. A. Richards has written of "stock responses," the automatic reactions people often have toward literature because of a preexisting set of attitudes. These attitudes tend to remove people from the actual experience of a literary work, substituting instead a biased vision, which may be positive or negative depending on the preexisting attitudes, but which in either case is a distortion. To borrow this terminology, we can say that *An Enemy of the People* is about stock responses to the truth. (The pun on "Stockmann" does not exist in the Norwegian.) The play is thus *not* a struggle between scientific enlightment and outmoded tradition. For that matter, no character specifically denies the baths' pollution; rather, they exaggerate, exploit, underestimate, or suppress it according to each one's individual bias. The newspapermen try to use it to overthrow the power structure of the town; when they learn that their tactic cannot work, they reverse their position. The Mayor, like many politicians today, evaluates a social problem solely in terms of money; for him, the amount of truth in his brother's discovery is inversely proportional to the expense of repairing the baths. Morten Kiil, Dr. Stockmann's father-in-law, sees the pollution as a threat to his reputation (the pollutants come from his tannery), and thus attempts to blackmail the pollution out of existence. The townspeople at the meeting in Act 4 are swayed not by a scientific discussion of water pollution, but rather by stock phrases like *moderation, the solid majority,* and *an enemy of the people,* emotional stimuli that enable them to evade the unpleasant truth that Dr. Stockmann's discovery will cost them a good deal of money.

Thus, using the baths as the focal point of the play raises the satire to a much higher level than in *The League of Youth. Enemy* depicts characters who are not so much wicked as they are *interested*. Their sins are not mortal but venial; each is swayed in his actions by his own individual weakness, whether it be financial, social, political, or personal. Ibsen provides two good small examples of this from the townspeople, in the characterizations of Mrs. Busk, Petra's employer, and Mr. Vik, the owner of Captain Horster's ship. (Mrs. Busk is not even seen; Mr. Vik appears briefly at the town meeting.) After Dr. Stockmann had been declared "an enemy of the people," Mrs. Busk felt compelled to fire Petra from her teaching post:

> PETRA. Mrs. Busk gave me my notice, so I thought it better to leave at once.
> DR. STOCKMANN. You did the right thing!
> MRS. STOCKMANN. Who would have thought Mrs. Busk would prove such a poor human being!
> PETRA. Oh, Mother, she really isn't so bad. It was plain to see how miserable she felt. But she said she didn't dare not to. So I got fired. (Pp. 368-69)

Similarly, Mr. Vik fired Horster as captain of Mr. Vik's ship, not out of hatred but out of fear:

> DR. STOCKMANN. And there we have Mr. Vik—a merchant, a man of wealth, independent in every way—! What a disgrace!
> HORSTER. He's quite fair-minded otherwise. He said himself he'd gladly have retained me if he dared to—
> DR. STOCKMANN. But he didn't dare? No, naturally!
> HORSTER. It's not so easy, he was telling me, when you belong to a party— (P. 371)

Dr. Stockmann typically storms and rages in self-righteous fashion, but the point is that both Mrs. Busk and Mr. Vik are decent enough people who are caught in a web. They are not mere personifications of "reaction"; they are instead just ordinary, nice people trying to survive.

Dr. Stockmann himself is no exception to the rule of self-interest. Like Ibsen's other social plays, *An Enemy of the People* is a family play. Dr. Stockmann's immediate family is a source of support for him (although his wife wavers a bit at first), leading to the ironic tableau at the end, but counterpoised against this family grouping are his other two close relatives, his brother and his father-in-law, who are his principal antagonists. The conflict in the play becomes a family feud as well as a political struggle. The fact that Ibsen makes the two leading characters in the play brothers (which is not at all essential in terms of the play's surface action) is extremely important. Dr. Stockmann's former life is the key to his true motivation: he was clearly a failure as a doctor,[7] describing his early days as an exile from his home town, "in the far north, at the dead end of nowhere" (p. 353). Meanwhile, his brother, having become Mayor of the town, was a success. But after returning home, Dr. Stockmann saw the opportunity to surpass him in the eyes of the townspeople by suggesting the installation of the baths. Instead, he saw his brother take over his idea, "put it into practical reality" (p. 286), become chairman of the board of the baths (p. 290), and ignore his advice on the installation of the waterpipes (p. 300). The motivation for Dr. Stockmann's furtive behavior, his crowing over his brother when he thinks he has the upper hand, and his masochistic seeking of martyrdom when he realizes that he is losing out to his brother again, as he has done all his life, is thoroughly established. The family struggle between the successful and unsuccessful brothers, a modern Jacob and Esau, is an underlying action of the play; at that level, the issue of the polluted baths is merely a catalyst.

The conflict between the brothers is most obvious in the scene in the newspaper office, at the end of Act 3, when Dr. Stockmann commandeers the Mayor's hat and stick and parades about, saying, "Some respect, if you will, Peter. I'm the authority in town now" (p. 342). Obviously, what is going on here is more than political; Dr. Stockmann's glee is the result of his supposing that he has at last defeated his hated older brother. But other scenes between the Doctor and the Mayor also crackle with brotherly rivalry. Right from the first act, even before the baths' pollution is established, they "fly at each other" (p.

290). They attack one another's character as only members of the same family can do: in Act 2, the Mayor calls Dr. Stockmann "thoughtless," "restless," "unruly," "combative," "irritable," "troublesome" (pp. 316-17)—all perfectly true! Dr. Stockmann ripostes in Act 4, calling his brother "slow of wit and thick of head" (p. 354), and lumping him together with "that wheezing, little, narrow-chested pack of reactionaries" (p. 356). They have much in common, these two brothers. Both are named "stokk"; both are abusive, vain, stubborn, self-righteous, and self-seeking. In a play that has quite a bit to say about heredity (I shall comment upon Dr. Stockmann's Darwinism shortly), the two brothers have acquired similar traits. But on a symbolic level, this is once again Ibsen's character-mirroring technique in operation. The Mayor is not only Dr. Stockmann's brother, but also his alter ego; he is a reflection of the worst side of Dr. Stockmann's character.

The character-mirroring technique explains not only the dramatic function of the Mayor, but of the strange, silent character, Captain Horster. Except for his supplying the house for the public meeting in Act 4, Horster seems extraneous to the action of the play. He is onstage for long periods of time without doing or saying anything. In contrast with nearly everyone else in the play, he seems to have no opinion on the polluted baths, nor indeed on any political issue:

> MRS. STOCKMANN. Are you sailing soon, Captain Horster?
> HORSTER. I think we'll be ready by next week.
> MRS. STOCKMANN. And you'll be going to America then?
> HORSTER. That's the intention, yes.
> BILLING. But then you can't vote in the new town election.
> HORSTER. There's an election coming up?
> BILLING. Didn't you know?

HORSTER. No, I don't bother with such things.
BILLING. But you *are* concerned about public affairs, aren't you?
HORSTER. No. I don't understand them.
BILLING. Even so, a person at least ought to vote.
HORSTER. People who don't understand, too?
BILLING. Understand? What do you mean by that? Society's like a ship: all hands have to stand to the wheel.
HORSTER. Maybe on land; but at sea it wouldn't work too well. (P. 293)

This terse exchange in Act 1 foreshadows Dr. Stockmann's "the majority is never right" speech in Act 4. Elsewhere in Act 4, Dr. Stockmann mentions that one of his ancestors was a pirate (p. 196), reinforcing the association between himself and Horster, the sea captain. It is noteworthy, too, that Horster makes his first entrance along with Dr. Stockmann in Act 1, without much introduction or description; more or less shadows Dr. Stockmann whenever he is onstage thereafter, quietly offering his assistance when needed; is disgraced and loses his ship as a result of this support (although unlike Dr. Stockmann he makes no fuss about it); and is the only character (aside from members of the Doctor's immediate family) to remain with Dr. Stockmann at the end. Horster is the exception to the rule of self-interest in the play. His quiet, courageous individualism contrasts with the Mayor's noisy, cowardly demagoguery, and reflects the ethical side of Dr. Stockmann. The Mayor and Horster, taken together, are an objectification of the ambiguity in Dr. Stockmann: the Doctor is self-seeking like his brother, yet idealistic like Horster; headstrong and impulsive like his brother, yet firm and unswerving under pressure like Horster; narrow-minded and provincial like his brother, yet on the side of truth like Horster. One recalls *Brand,* in which a worldly Mayor is contrasted with the idealistic Brand, who even captains a boat in the second act. In *An Enemy of the People,* the politician and the ship-captain, the manipulator and the solitary leader, the aesthetic man of the people and the ethical "enemy of the people," unite in a single character.

As in the earlier plays, all the characters in *Enemy* can be charted in Kierkegaardian terms:

AESTHETIC	Ironic	ETHICAL
	Dr. Stockmann	Captain Horster
Mayor (gradually exposed)	◄───────────	Mayor (beginning)
	(Mayor throughout)	
	Aslaksen	
Hovstad (Acts 3-5)	◄───────────	Hovstad (1-2)
	(Hovstad throughout)	
Billing (3-5)	◄───────────	Billing (1-2)
	(Billing throughout)	
Mrs. Stockmann		Petra Stockmann
Eilif Stockmann (pagan)		Morten Stockmann (Christian)
The Drunk	Townspeople	Mr. Rørland (Pastor)
	Morten Kiil	
	Mr. Vik, Mrs. Busk	
	Landlord	
	Randina (maid)	
	Stensgaard (mentioned)	

The abundance of names in the center column reflects the fact that the principal focus in this play is on the ironic life. A large number of characters reflect Dr. Stockmann directly, just as others, like Horster or the Mayor, reflect aspects of him. The arrows in the chart once again represent changes in character, which in this play are through exposure rather than transformation. Like Helmer in *A Doll House,* the Mayor seems decent enough when we first see him in Act 1. He is concerned for the welfare of the town, and of his brother; he is also frugal and self-denying, refusing to take food or drink at his brother's extravagant table: "I'll stick to my bread and butter and tea. It's healthier in the long run—and a bit more economical, too" (p. 284). He speaks to Dr. Stockmann in high-minded, moralistic terms:

> You have an inveterate tendency to go your own way, in any case. And in a well-ordered society, that's nearly as inexcusable. The individual has to learn to subordinate himself to the whole—or, I should say, to those authorities charged with the common good. (P. 291)

But the split in the final sentence is the key to his exposure. Although he seems to be talking about the individual's subordination to principle, he actually means subordination to "authorities charged with the common good," which is to say, to him, personally. By Act 4, when he harangues the crowd, we see him as an unprincipled demagogue, manipulating the townspeople entirely for the sake of his personal profit and vanity. In Kierkegaardian terms, he is not ethical but aesthetic, not a leader but merely a persuader, not a Brand but a Peer Gynt. Because of hypocrisy, we might place him, like his brother, in the "ironic" column throughout, but his ironic nature is different from that of Dr. Stockmann. Dr. Stockmann is a new type of ironic man for Ibsen, seeming to embody the extremes of aesthetic and ethical with ease, while the Mayor is of the old type, an artificial, uneasy juxtaposition lacking in validity. And, oddly enough, the two brothers are a reversal of the situation in *Ghosts:* where Manders, the unconscious hypocrite, was shown to be worse than Engstrand, the conscious one, now Dr. Stockmann, totally unaware of the contradictions in his own character, is depicted as better than his cunning, self-cognizant brother.

The three newspapermen, Aslaksen, Hovstad, and Billing are similar to the Mayor, and to one another. But there is no exposure in the case of Aslaksen. His repetitious catchword, "moderation," expresses his middle position from the beginning. Furthermore, moderation is not a principle for him, but rather an evasion of principle. He urges moderation only when extremism might hurt his business; in the pivotal crowd scene, he never asks for moderation from the Mayor or the townspeople, even though they become more extreme in attacking Dr. Stockmann than the Doctor himself ever was in attacking the baths or the power structure of the town. But if anything, Hovstad and Billing, Aslaksen's two muckraking journalists, are even worse than Aslaksen. Aslaksen owns the paper, which gives a financial justification for his behavior; nothing would be gained, for either him or Dr. Stockmann, if *The People's Courier* went out of business. Aslaksen's "moderation," though petty, is at least motivated. But Hovstad and Billing would hardly have their careers destroyed for standing behind Dr. Stockmann, even if they were driven out of town; if anything, the scandal would probably enhance their reputations. There is something *casual* about their abrupt shift from alliance with the Doctor to alliance with the Mayor. They blow with the prevailing winds.

Billing is in one sense the worse of the two, and in another sense the better. His name expresses his character, suggesting the Norwegian word *billig* (cheap). In the opening scene of the play, we see him established as a man of appetite:

> MRS. STOCKMANN. Well, if you come an hour late, Mr. Billing, then you have to accept cold food.
> BILLING *(eating)*. It tastes simply marvelous—just perfect.
> MRS. STOCKMANN. Because you know how precise my husband is about keeping his regular mealtime—
> BILLING. Doesn't bother me in the least. In fact, I really think food tastes best to me when I can eat like this, alone and undisturbed.

MRS. STOCKMANN. Yes, well—just so you enjoy it. (P. 283)

He is gobbling down the Doctor's food in the same way that he soon starts to gobble down his ideas, but when those ideas start to taste indigestible, he spits them out. Dr. Stockmann's carefulness about mealtimes suggests that his appetites, at least, are regulated, but Billing is concerned only with having a good feed; he does not care about the time, and is cheerily unaware that he is both exploiting the Doctor's hospitality by dining alone and insulting him by saying he prefers it that way. Billing is a Gyntian creature, true only to his animal self. Later in the first act, at the prompting of Dr. Stockmann's two sons, he loudly proclaims himself a pagan:

> MORTEN. Mr. Rørland says that work is a punishment for our sins.
> EILIF *(snorts)* Pah, how stupid you are, to believe that stuff.
> MRS. STOCKMANN. Now, now, Eilif!
> BILLING *(laughing).* Oh, marvelous.
> HOVSTAD. You'd rather not work so hard, Morten?
> MORTEN. No, I wouldn't.
> HOVSTAD. Yes, but what do you want to be in life?
> MORTEN. Best of all, I want to be a Viking.
> EILIF. But then you'd have to be a pagan.
> MORTEN. Well, so then I'll be a pagan.
> BILLING. I'm with you, Morten! Exactly what I say!
> MRS. STOCKMANN *(making signals).* No, you don't really, Mr. Billing.
> BILLING. Ye gods, yes—! I *am* a pagan, and proud of it. (Pp. 295-96)

This split between paganism and Christianity is the same as in Ibsen's *Emperor and Galilean,* with the former standing for the aesthetic life of pleasure and self-indulgence and the latter for the ethical life of duty and self-restraint. In this sense, Billing's "paganism" can be taken literally. Even before the Mayor wins him over to his side, we learn that Billing has "put in for a job in the town clerk's office" (p. 329). His muckraking is a complete sham; he is really a pagan, and his only principle might be that of the troll king in *Peer Gynt:* "to thine own self be enough."

Hovstad, as shown in the quotation, maintains a stronger ethical façade than Billing does, through the first three acts. It is in this sense that he is worse than Billing, who with his boisterousness, his eating and drinking, his lively outspokenness, and his carefree attitudes, has all the charm typical of Ibsen's Gyntian characters. The audience sees through Billing from the beginning, which makes his conversion to reactionism not only understandable but predictable. But Hovstad's shift in alliance comes as a shock. Up until the moment in the third act when the Mayor points out the economic disaster that would result from admitting that the baths are polluted, Hovstad seems every inch the nineteenth-century moralist, denouncing Aslaksen's spinelessness, while urging Dr. Stockmann on. It is even Hovstad who first puts the idea into Dr. Stockmann's head that the pollution of the baths is a symbol of much broader political and moral issues:

> That's why I want to take this opportunity now and see if I can't force some of these models of intention to make men of themselves for once. The worship of authority in this town has to be uprooted. This inexcusable lapse of judgment about the water system has to be driven home to every eligible voter. (P. 311)

But all this moralism turns out to be just as much an outer shell as that of Torvald Helmer in *A Doll House* or the Mayor in this play. In the exchange with Billing and Aslaksen over the renegade Councilman Stensgaard,

Hovstad insists that "I'm no double-dealer—and I never will be" (p. 329), to which Aslaksen replies, "A politician has to keep all possibilities open, Mr. Hovstad" (p. 329). Hovstad does not object to being characterized as a "politician." Aslaksen is right, but in a way he does not realize. All *three* are double dealers—all "politicians," all Stensgaards—but Hovstad, in maintaining such a convincing façade of liberal morality, is the most duplicitous of all.

Morten Kiil, like the Mayor, is a "reflector" of Dr. Stockmann. He is of course related to the Doctor, as his father-in-law, and he shares the attributes common to this family group of irascibility and self-centeredness. He has precisely the same resentment against the town fathers that Dr. Stockmann has, having been excluded from membership on the town council:

> They think they're so much smarter than us old boys. They hounded me out of the town council. That's right, I'm telling you, like a dog they hounded me out, they did. But now they're going to get it. You just go on and lay your monkeyshines on them, Stockmann. (P. 304)

But Kiil is a much coarser version of the ironic type than Dr. Stockmann is. Kiil totally lacks scientific or philosophical insight; he even misinterprets Dr. Stockmann's statements about the pollution, and thinks it is all a joke about "animals" in the waterpipes. For him, the whole affair is *strictly* one of getting back at the town leaders—it never even occurs to him that the Doctor might actually be right. He has a kind of Gyntian vigor as he gloats over what he believes to be a wonderful practical joke; but his aesthetic side is counterbalanced by his obsession with money and reputation. When it appears that the "joke" will backfire on him (the pollution comes from his tannery), he takes the money that he had intended to leave in his will to Dr. Stockmann's family, and invests it in shares in the baths.

From that point, both men thus have a financial and personal interest in keeping the pollution covered up; Stockmann sticks to his original position where Kiil does not. Kiil thus shows what the Doctor could have been were his "ironic" character on a lower plane.

Within Dr. Stockmann's immediate family, the Kierkegaardian pattern is maintained in carefully balanced fashion. Mrs. Stockmann is motivated by a purely aesthetic love of her family, which is counterposed against the claims of duty:

> DR. STOCKMANN. Then anyway I'll have done my duty to the people—to society. Though they call me its enemy!
> MRS. STOCKMANN. And to your family, Thomas? To us at home? You think that's doing your duty to those who depend on you?
> PETRA. Oh, stop always thinking of us first of all, Mother.
> MRS. STOCKMANN. Yes, it's easy for *you* to talk. If need be, you can stand on your own feet. But remember the boys, Thomas. And think of yourself a little, and of me— (P. 322)

Although Mrs. Stockmann comes to support her husband, it is a support based on love rather than on principle. At one point, when Dr. Stockmann announces a plan to walk through the streets with a drummer, crying out the truth from every corner, her reaction is that "Morten would love to do it; and Eilif—he'll go along" (P. 345). She seems to see the issue entirely as a matter of a merry family outing! Her enthusiasm soon wanes, however, and although she remains devoted to her husband, she also remains frightened for him and the rest of her family right to the end of the play, while never having uttered a word on the social issues involved. Balanced against her mother is Petra, the oldest child, who chides her mother in the quotation above for her obsession with family. Petra stands behind her father's cause with admiration and support throughout the play. Her name means "rock"; she is solid, unchanging in her devotion to principle, a purely ethical type like Horster.

Dr. Stockmann's two young boys also seem balanced off against each other. Morten, as shown in the passage already quoted, is concerned with duty and religion, citing the town Pastor:

> MORTEN. You must be terribly wicked, Petra.
> PETRA. Wicked?
> MORTEN. Yes, when you work so hard. Mr. Rørland says that work is a punishment for our sins. (P. 295)

But Eilif, the other son, characterizes this attitude as "stupid"; it is he who says that he wants to be a Viking and a pagan, thus putting the idea into Billing's head (p. 295). And even Randina, the unseen maid, has a position in the Kierkegaardian scheme. All we know about her is that she has a "smudgy nose"; the running gag is that Dr. Stockmann can never remember her name, but can only think of her nose. Her dripping nose is meaningful in a play concerned with pollution; by the device of Dr. Stockmann's "Freudian slip" Ibsen seems to be suggesting a weakness in Dr. Stockmann with respect to dirty truths. He is not so clear sighted as he thinks he is, either in this small case or in the major one concerning the baths. At the same time, the idea of a servant with a dirty nose suggests a dual nature of the ironic type; on the one hand, she is devoted to duty (in this case merely the simple duty of cleaning up), but on the other hand, she lets herself go, being too lazy or filthy even to wipe her own nose. Thus Randina, like the Mayor and Morten Kiil, is a device for setting off the character of Dr. Stockmann, a "reflector" on a very small scale.

Ibsen's treatment of the minor characters, then, is as

usual very controlled. I have already discussed the characterizations of Mr. Vik and Mrs. Busk. Another important minor character is the drunk in the crowd scene, the only person among the townspeople to support the Doctor when a vote is taken to declare him an "enemy of the people." Drunkenness is of course characteristic of the aesthetic level. It is interesting that, outside Dr. Stockmann's immediate family, the only characters to support him are those who are purely aesthetic or purely ethical: the drunk and Captain Horster. (The reason there is only one vote for Dr. Stockmann is that the family does not vote, while Horster—true to his ethical nature as a loner—was established early on as never voting.)

The townspeople are depicted in equivocal fashion. When we actually see them, in Act 4, they are characterized simply as a raucous, mindless crowd. The stage directions call for their "confusion, outcries, and laughter" (p. 354), "laughter, commotion, and whistles" (p. 354), "wild turmoil, ... shouting, stamping, and whistling" (p. 355). They are simply a mob, a herd, "the raw material out of which a people is shaped" (p. 358), as Dr. Stockmann puts it, or, in other words, at Kierkegaard's aesthetic level. They recall the strident crowds of trolls and monkeys in *Peer Gynt.* Yet their aestheticism is not so pure as that of the drunk, whom they keep expelling from the meeting; moblike though they may be, they maintain a sense of propriety, as well as a keen sense of their financial self-interest. They react violently when the Mayor reminds them that Dr. Stockmann's proposal "would actually mean afflicting our local taxpayers with a needless expenditure of at least a hundred thousand crowns" (p. 350). And the subject of drink comes up again at the end of the scene, in a collection of priggish remarks about the Doctor:

> ANOTHER GENTLEMAN (*to* BILLING). Say, you've visited there off and on. Have you noticed if the man drinks?

> BILLING. Ye gods, I don't know what to say. When anybody stops in, there's always toddy on the table.
> A THIRD GENTLEMAN. No, I think at times he's just out of his mind.
> FIRST GENTLEMAN. I wonder if there isn't a strain of insanity in the family? (P. 363)

Like the newspapermen, the townspeople have dual natures; if they are a herd, they are a respectable, snobbish, bourgeois one.

But there is a deeper sense in which the townspeople are presented as ironic. The dilemma, the ambiguity of democracy, is summed up in Hovstad's rationalization to the crowd:

> I make no claim of any kind of distinction. I was born of simple peasants, and I'm proud that my roots run deep in those masses that he despises. (P. 360)

Hovstad has become a man of the people, and Dr. Stockmann an "enemy of the people." Which is the proper attitude, for a person of humane and progressive views, toward the masses? Should one be a leader or merely a persuader, a Brand or a Peer Gynt? Is the majority always right, as Hovstad insists, and must one follow it even when it appears obviously wrong, as in our own time with the Vietnam war? Radicals are always invoking "the people" as the source of all that is good and true; wickedness in political affairs comes only from "politicians," who have somehow managed to circumvent "the people." But "the people" in this sense are often all too passive and pliable, "the silent majority" who are aware of only their immediate self-interest, and who are susceptible to the first demagogue who plays on those interests. The characterization of Hovstad is an important lesson for those who are willing to take it. Democracy can be either good or evil, can produce either a Pericles or a Cleon, a Roosevelt or a

Hitler, a Dr. Stockmann or a Mayor Stockmann. "The solid majority" can be either aesthetic or ethical, either a "mass" or a "people."

Ibsen has thus chosen an element from modern life that is *inherently* symbolic of Kierkegaard's ironic level. The same can be said of the other symbolic elements of the play; like the townspeople, the scenic and imagistic elements, while perfectly realistic, automatically carry with them meanings that are ambiguous. Consider the settings, for example. Northam has denounced these as containing few examples of visual suggestion. But the opening act is placed in one of Ibsen's typical foreground/background sets,[8] with Dr. Stockmann's living room in front and the dining room at the back. In the living room, ethical discussions take place over the baths, the town's economy, and its political power structure. In the background, in the dining room, Billing sits stuffing himself with roast beef. We are shown from the first moment that the issues in this play are not pure, that they take place against a background of *appetite*.

Act 2 has the same setting as the first, but the stage directions specify that "the dining room door is closed" (p. 302). This act consists primarily of the debate between Dr. Stockmann and his brother the Mayor. We seem to be moving away, then, from the appetite-dominated background of the first act into an ethical world of pure discussion. Subsequent changes of scene, however, symbolize the shifting movements of plot away from the purely ethical. Kenneth Burke has written of the settings of *An Enemy of the People* as illustrations of his concept of the "Scene-Act Ratio," the way in which the scenic background "both *realistically reflects* the course of the action and *symbolizes* it."[9] Thus, Burke points out:

> Act III takes place in the editorial office of the People's Messenger, a local newspaper in which Dr. Stockmann had hoped to publish his evidence that the

water supply was contaminated. The action takes on a more forensic reference, in keeping with the nature of the place. . . .

In the next Act Dr. Stockmann does contrive to lay his case before a public tribunal of a sort: a gathering of fellow-townsmen, assembled in "a big old-fashioned room," in the house of a friend. His appeal is unsuccessful; his neighbors vote overwhelmingly against him, and the scene ends in turbulence. As regards the scene-act ratio, note that the semi-public, semi-intimate setting reflects perfectly the quality of Dr. Stockmann's appeal.

In Act V, the stage directions tell us that the hero's clothes are torn, and the room is in disorder, with broken windows. You may consider these details either as properties of the scene or as a reflection of the hero's condition after his recent struggle with the forces of reaction. The scene is laid in Dr. Stockmann's *study,* a setting so symbolic of the direction taken by the plot that the play ends with Dr. Stockmann announcing his plan to enroll twelve young *disciples* and with them to found a *school* in which he will work for the *education* of society.[10]

In addition to Burke's excellent perceptions, one might point out that in all three cases the settings tend to have an *ironic* function, in both the Kierkegaardian and the usual senses of the word. Billing's eating of roast beef in Act 1 while serious political matters are discussed, or the final tableau in which Dr. Stockmann's ringing words about standing alone are belied by the surrounding presence of his family and Captain Horster, are but examples of the general trend for the settings ironically to undercut the action. The disorder in Act 5 not only reflects the hero's condition after his recent struggle; it, like Stockmann's torn pants, reflects the disorder in the Doctor's own character. Act 3, the newspaper office, is described as similarly disordered:

> At the center of the room is a large table covered with papers, newspapers, and books. . . . The room is barren

and cheerless, the furnishings old, the armchairs grimy and torn. (P. 324)

This disorder suggests the weakness in the characters of the newspapermen, and is a constant reminder of it as the scene progresses. At the same time, this is also a double setting: At the back, one can see the pressroom, where "two typesetters can be seen at work, and, beyond them, a handpress [seen] in operation" (p. 324). The ambiguity of the first act has been reversed: now the ethical, businesslike level is in the background, while the selfish behavior—the betrayal of Dr. Stockmann's cause—has moved to the foreground.

Finally, the "semi-public" nature of the setting in Act 4 is perfect for expressing the central ambivalence of the play toward democracy versus individualism. It is Horster's home, and thus expressive of the individual, yet it becomes the house of the mob. The scenic backgrounds in the play, then, can be charted in a manner similar to that of the characters:

	AESTHETIC	Ironic	ETHICAL
Acts 1 & 2:	Dining Room	← Dr. Stockmann's house →	Living room
Act 3:	Editorial Office	← Newspaper office →	Pressroom
Act 4:	Crowd	← Horster's house →	Horster
Act 5:	Broken windows, torn trousers, general disorder	← Dr. Stockmann's study →	Bookcases, cabinets, books, papers, medicines

I have tried to depict in this chart the fact that the scenic backgrounds either embody extremes within themselves, or are literally split into two parts.

In similar fashion, the major physical elements of the play, and the major verbal imagery, are ambiguous; they either have opposing connotations built into them, or are paired off in contrasting opposites:

THE VALIDITY OF THE IRONIC LIFE / 173

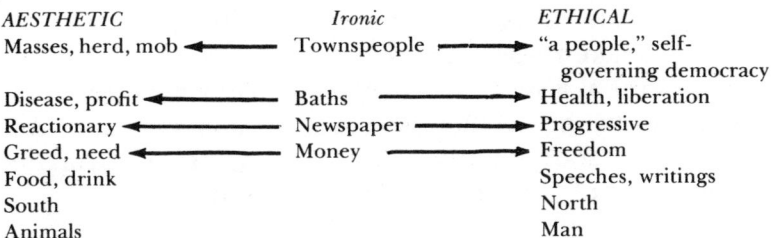

AESTHETIC	Ironic	ETHICAL
Masses, herd, mob ←	Townspeople →	"a people," self-governing democracy
Disease, profit ←	Baths →	Health, liberation
Reactionary ←	Newspaper →	Progressive
Greed, need ←	Money →	Freedom
Food, drink		Speeches, writings
South		North
Animals		Man

The townspeople are a scenic as well as a physical and verbal element of the play; in Act 4, as the crowd, they are an important part of the scenic background. Perhaps influenced by the Duke of Saxe-Meiningen, the innovative German stage director who put his best actors in his crowds and orchestrated them with precision (and who produced many of Ibsen's plays, and presented Ibsen himself with a medal), Ibsen created a crowd full of precise satirical portraits, whose reactions must be carefully scored. One must remember that the standard practice in the nineteenth-century had been to hire extras on the day of performance, who did little more than fill up space. Indeed, crowds were sometimes created by painting them on the backdrop! By contrast, Ibsen's mob presents a severe challenge for actors and stage director. The crowd is extremely rowdy, yet individualized; their reaction cannot be just general uproar, but a growing rage in reaction to what is being said. In the beginning of the act, they arrive in small groups, individually characterized as "gentlemen," "workmen," "schoolboys," and so on; several are given names, such as "Lamstad," or "Skipper Evensen" (p. 346). As the act proceeds, however, there is a careful progression; there is more and more disorder, requiring "shouting above the noise" (p. 361), as the townspeople lose their individualities and become a herd of screaming animals. The relationship between the masses and the people that Dr. Stockmann describes—"The masses are . . .

the raw material out of which a people is shaped" (p. 358)—has taken place in reverse.

The baths as a symbol undergo a similar transformation, but more abruptly. When we first hear about them in Act 1, they are a source not only of health for those partaking of them, but of "health" for the town itself:

> We have our great, new, magnificent installation, the spa. Mark my words, Mr. Hovstad—these baths will become the very life-principle of our town.... Why, it's simply extraordinary the way this place has revived in the past two years! People here have some money again. There's life, excitement! Land and property values are rising every day. (P. 285)

In the nineteenth century, spas were much more highly valued for their health-giving properties than they are today (although even now they have their fanatical adherents). The sudden shift when the baths are shown to be polluted, a source rather than a cure for disease, would thus have carried great emotional weight for an audience of the time. But the ambivalency of newspapers, as of money, is a timeless quality that requires no imaginative return to the nineteenth century to appreciate. Very few of our supposedly liberal publications emerged with unclean hands from their coverage of Vietnam or Watergate; the New York *Times*, the Washington *Post*, et al. maintain a simultaneously adverse and cooperative relationship with government exactly like that of *The People's Courier* toward the town government in *An Enemy of the People*. They will attack individual evils, but they will not attack the whole system, the power structure of society.

And of course money has always been known for its ability both to liberate and to enslave. It appears in the play that the new money has freed the town from its backwardness, its unemployment, and its stagnation; but the threat of its loss shows that money has actually become a cruel tyrant, a necessity to be protected at all costs. Dr. Stockmann at the beginning of the play is shown as having, for the first time in his life, a surplus of money, enabling him to be extravagant in opening up his house, in having rich food and drink and cigars, and, most important, to be extravagant in promulgating ideas. At the end of the play, however, we see him as having lost the sources of all this extravagance—the support of the town (and thus his patients), plus his wife's inheritance. Money enabled him to speak his mind; now money, or rather moneyed interests, will prevent him. Very few plays are as blunt about economics as this one (as Bertolt Brecht once pointed out, money is far more often a dirty secret on stage than is sex), which boldly shows the universal power, the inescapability, of money over people's lives. Behind all the speeches and editorials in the play, the talk of science and reaction and politics, lies the necessity of food and drink and shelter; and behind them all lies the great ambivalent reality of money.

Two motifs of imagery are worth discussing. First, as usual for Ibsen, there is the pattern of North versus South, standing, respectively, for the ethical and the aesthetic levels. In this case, however, there has been an overall shift northward: the town, although in Norway, is now "south." North has become the far north, the town in which Dr. Stockmann spent his years in exile, in "that waste of rocks" (p. 353). By contrast, Dr. Stockmann's home town represents to him (at least at first) all the vitality that Italy did for Nora or Paris did for Osvald:

> You can just imagine how tight things were for us up there, yes, many times. And now we can live like kings! (P. 289)

Dr. Stockmann revels in his new, warm home, his roast beef, his hot toddy, even his table cloth and his lamp shade (pp. 288-89). But by the final act, when we see Dr. Stockmann in his torn pants standing in his dreary, devastated study, the locale has taken on all the aspects that Ibsen traditionally associated with Norway: deprivation, coldness, narrowness, bigotry.

The second major imagery pattern, reminiscent of *Peer Gynt,* is that of animals. In Act 4 alone, there are references to a lion, an eider duck, a pack of goats, barnyard fowl, a crow, a raven, a hen, a pheasant, a turkey, dogs (several times), and vermin. Morten Kiil is called "the badger," and as a tanner he engages in the treatment of animal skins. Kiil's concept of the water pollution is that "little animals got loose in the waterpipes" (p. 304); he says that he was "hounded" *(hundsvoterte)* out of the town council "like a dog," and asks his son-in-law to lay "monkeyshines" *(abespil,* literally "monkey game") on the other councillors, and to "make monkeys out of them" (p. 304). Elsewhere, there are casual metaphors involving spiders, jellyfish, birds of passage, a fox, wolves, a pig. As in *Peer Gynt,* animals stand for the aesthetic life, but there is an added element in Ibsen's infusion of Darwinism into the play. Dr. Stockmann, in Act 4, puts forth an evolutionary view of society that is pure social Darwinism: "the majority is never right," but instead, "the right is with me, and the other few, the solitary individuals" (p. 356). Ideas evolve in a similar fashion:

> An ordinary, established truth lives, as a rule—let's say—some seventeen, eighteen, at the most twenty years; rarely more. . . . The truths accepted by the masses now are the ones proclaimed basic by the advance guard in our grandfathers' time. We fighters on the frontiers today, we no longer recognize them. (Pp. 356-57)

Later in the scene, Dr. Stockmann develops an elaborate metaphor about the breeding of animals to make his point about the truth residing with advanced, superior individuals; when one of the townspeople protests that "we're not animals, Doctor!" Stockmann replies:

> Oh yes, brother, we *are* animals! We're the best animals, all in all, that any man could wish for. But there aren't many animals of quality among us. There's a terrible gap between the thoroughbreds and the mongrels in humanity. (P. 359)

This might have come straight out of Herbert Spencer, as might the following exchange in Act 5:

> DR. STOCKMANN. If I don't bail out the *Courier,* you'll put a vile construction on it all. You'll hound me down—set upon me—try to choke me off like a dog chokes a hare!
> HOVSTAD. That's the law of nature. Every animal has to struggle for survival. (P. 381)

As if taking Hovstad's advice, Dr. Stockmann goes on to change his tactics; at the end of the play, instead of contemptuously rejecting "mongrels," as he did in Act 4, Stockmann now says, "I want to experiment with mongrels for a change" (p. 385). These mongrels, the street boys whom Dr. Stockmann will turn into his disciples, have proved their ability to survive. Thus, in the struggle against reaction, the "fittest" may be these unlikely young outcasts, in the same way that Dr. Stockmann could become a hero despite being an unlikely misfit himself.

All this Darwinism adds to the moral ambiguity that forms the play's ambience. A "mass" can become a "people"; even mongrels can develop into superior individuals. Most important, from a herd of townspeople, an enlightened hero like Dr. Stockmann can evolve. This is a different idea from any in the earlier plays. Brand, for example, is in no way a man of the people, and apparently never has been. Ethical people do not "evolve" out of the aesthetic, either for Kierkegaard or for the earlier Ibsen; they change drastically, like Nora Helmer. Unlike Dr. Stockmann, they leave no trace of their former, aesthetic selves. Darwinism is a distinctly un-Kierkegaardian philosophy, in which species develop gradually rather than abruptly, out of an interaction with their environment rather than entirely from within.

It is this Darwinist viewpoint that enables Ibsen to portray, for the first time, an intermediate, "ironic" hero, having a valid existence. In Dr. Stockmann, we recognize a modern, realistic protagonist, like Strindberg's Miss Julie, who is described so elaborately in the preface to that play.[11] Like Miss Julie, Dr. Stockmann is neither good nor bad. He is multifaceted, mixing noble and base impulses, and developing out of a complex of formative pressures—the rivalries of his childhood; his need for fame, his native stubbornness, his experience of poverty and hardship; his love of money, comfort, food, and drink; and his scientific and intellectual talents.

Thus, *An Enemy of the People* is a pivotal play for Ibsen. Dr. Stockmann prepares the way for the complex characters in the later plays, such as Gregers Werle, Rebekka West, Hedda Gabler, or Halvard Solness. Such characters are the sort that both audiences and actors have since come to prefer—intricate, realistic, well-rounded, "modern." Unlike Ibsen's earlier creations, they cannot be understood as simple types at discrete levels; their qualities are multiple, their motives often unclear even to themselves. Nevertheless, a preference for multifaceted characters should not blind us to the values of the earlier plays in which the characters are but simple types. In those plays, as I have tried to demonstrate, *complexity of play is the substitute for complexity of individual.* The play taken as a whole has the intricacy that is later distilled into a single personage. And the greatness of *An Enemy of the People* is that it offers both: a complex central character set in a play that has perfectly controlled, abstractly patterned supporting characters and surrounding detail.

7 / Reflections on Art and Politics

ONE of the great controversies of our century is over the relationship between art and politics. Theater, in particular, has been involved in the debate, some maintaining that "drama is a weapon," and others that dramatic art shrivels wherever it is touched by practical or social problems. This extreme polarity is the reason for the constant flip-flopping of Ibsen's reputation that I have discussed in this book.

The difficulty that so many people have in getting a grasp on the problem of art and politics comes from an inadequate view of how art functions. The artistic process is improperly conceived as a simple diad of artist-audience. The artist creates a "message," which he transmits directly to the audience via his art work; the work itself is thus merely a passive conduit for philosophical ideas. The question of artistic value is reduced to one of the quality of the message. Thus, transitory problems like water pollution or syphilis cannot possibly be the proper subject matter for great works of art, which must of necessity deal with lofty eternals. Ibsen's social plays are disqualified from the start. Or, conversely, the artist's message *must* deal with social problems, must fight suffering and injustice, rather than indulge in escapist dreaming. Ibsen's social plays are excellent, but they must be updated, adapted, made more propagandist. Both points of view end up with little respect for the plays as written.

The way out of this double bind is to view the process of

artistic communication triadically, as Jakobson did with his famous scheme. Artistic communication is not merely the dyad of artist-audience but the triad of artist-work-audience. In drama, the play is not a mere neutral transmitter, passing on ideas directly from playwright to audience member; instead, the play itself is "foregrounded." We become aware of it for its own sake. With a good play, there is no sensation that the playwright is *telling* us something; instead, the play seems to *live,* apart from both us and the playwright. This is what Bertolt Brecht realized in positing his famous "Alienation Effect." In order to avoid simplistic agitprop on the one hand, and Romantic escapism on the other, he proposed a process whereby the social content of drama is "estranged," or objectified. The playwright does not speak directly to the audience, but instead creates a play that is detached; the audience is thus not manipulated or propagandized, but instead finds its own relationship with the work of art. Meaning is *found* in the work rather than transmitted directly by it; the audience responds to the work as a whole, as with a living organism, rather than to its "ideas" in piecemeal fashion. The process universalizes those ideas, even when they are transient ones. Thus a modern person, fully democratic in his beliefs, can respond to a play like Shakespeare's *Richard II*, even though the divine right of kings is a politically dead issue. Similarly, even when women become the full equals of men in our society, *A Doll House* will still be a great play because it objectifies the feminist problems of the nineteenth century, rather than trying to stimulate us with them directly. Anyone (even a man) can identify with Nora's problems, because Ibsen's technique universalizes them. This does not mean that he makes them so general that they are "relevant" for all time, but rather that he renders them so vivid, and so clearly structured, that audiences of all time can have emotional access to them.

His "message" is not universal in itself, but rather is *made* universal.

For Bertolt Brecht, the "estrangement," or universalization, was often accomplished by external, technical means, such as slides, films, songs, or masks. For Ibsen, I have tried to show that the estrangement, while incorporating theatrical elements like props and setting, is a more organic process. The realistic elements are arranged in a kind of mosaic, enabling us both to respond emotionally and to understand objectively. Nora does not just show us her problems directly, but also has them objectified by being set in a Kierkegaardian pattern that transforms the "problems" into a work of art. The play is thus not a piecemeal collection of people and ideas that harangue the audience like a sermon; it is instead an interconnected process. The result is both politics *and* art, or rather, politics *become* art. It is not any the less powerful for having become objectified. On the contrary, its effect is more lasting. Audiences may not rush out into the street after a performance to start a revolution (which never really happens with agitprop either), but an inner revolution, slower but surer than with agitprop, has been set up. If the issues in the play are still current, it becomes a focal point for discussion, questioning, argument; if not, it performs the no less important function of opening up the audience's imagination, of taking them into a past world and making it live again. In the jargon of today, the audience undergoes a "change of consciousness," becoming more sensitive and open to human problems generally.

It goes without saying that if this effect is to be achieved, the plays must be produced with their patterns intact. One cannot lift stones out of a mosaic and expect them to be very important by themselves. Unfortunately, our theater today is still dominated by the attitudes of traditional, piecemeal dramatic criticism, and tends to do just that.

Adaptations, alterations, revisions, or "updatings" of classical plays are the exception rather than the rule, reflecting an erroneous belief that one can change parts of a play without altering the whole.

Despite the extensive critical revaluation of Ibsen, he continues to have a low reputation in the practical theater. He is not produced as often as he should be. (One recent survey of university productions revealed that Ibsen was not even among the top fourteen most frequently produced playwrights; he lags behind not only Shakespeare, but also Neil Simon, Noel Coward, and Thornton Wilder.)[1] But even worse, when his plays are produced, they tend to appear in adaptations that are as awkward and vulgar as those perpetrated on Shakespeare. The most common version of *An Enemy of the People* to be produced in English is Arthur Miller's simplistic adaptation of 1950; two recent films of *A Doll House* both altered the text to make it more feminist; a promising stage version of *Hedda Gabler* with a famous director and first-rate actors turned out to have a drastically altered setting and a graceless version of the script. And so it goes; Ibsen's reputation as a fussy and outdated propagandist still remains in the theater, causing directors to alter his scripts, with results that lower Ibsen's reputation still further.

The mistake is to think that his plays need to be improved in order to work in the contemporary theater. Any director who treats Ibsen seriously as a practical playwright will discover how tightly structured his scripts are, with every physical detail charged with significance, and with a sense of tempo, rhythm, and progression that is unmatched by any contemporary playwright. I have never seen or read an adaptation of an Ibsen play that came anywhere near the original in vigor and import. The best possible result that this book could achieve would be to stimulate some productions of Ibsen's middle plays by the major theater companies of the world. Such productions would reject the simple-minded propaganda approach of the ubiquitous "adaptations," and instead respect Ibsen's plays as subtle, complex, connected works of art.

Notes

Chapter 1: A Structuralist Approach to Ibsen

1. Roman Jakobson, "Linguistics and Poetics," in *Style in Language*, ed. Thomas A. Sebeok (Cambridge, Mass.: M.I.T. Press, 1960), pp. 350-77. (This essay has been widely reprinted.)
2. Orley I. Holtan, *Mythic Patterns in Ibsen's Late Plays* (Minneapolis: University of Minnesota Press, 1970), p. 35.
3. Charles R. Lyons, *Henrik Ibsen: The Divided Consciousness* (Carbondale and Edwardsville: Southern Illinois University Press, 1972).
4. John Northam, *Ibsen: A Critical Study* (Cambridge: Cambridge University Press, 1973).
5. John Northam, *Ibsen's Dramatic Method* (London: Faber and Faber, 1953), p. 85.
6. Roland Barthes, *S/Z* (Paris: Éditions du Seuil, 1970).
7. Henrik Ibsen, *Letters of Henrik Ibsen*, trans. John Nilsen Laurvik and Mary Morison (New York: Duffield & Co., 1908), p. 199.
8. Eva Le Gallienne, "Ibsen, the Shy Giant," *Saturday Review* 54, no. 33 (August 14, 1971): 23.
9. Brian Johnston, *The Ibsen Cycle* (Boston: G. K. Hall, 1975), p. 2.
10. Ibid., p. 10.
11. Jan Mukařovský, *Structure, Sign, and Function*, trans. and ed. John Burbank and Peter Steiner (New Haven and London: Yale University Press, 1978), p. 50.
12. Ibid., p. 52.
13. Johnston, *Ibsen Cycle*, p. 14.

Chapter 2: Ibsen's Allegorical Realism

1. Northam, *Ibsen: A Critical Study*, pp. 6-7.
2. G. Wilson Knight, *Henrik Ibsen* (New York: Grove, 1962), p. 48.
3. Erich Auerbach, *Mimesis: The Representation of Reality in Western Literature* (Princeton, N.J.: Princeton University Press, 1953), pp. 6-7. Auerbach's use of the word *rhythmic* here shows that *continuous* does not mean uniformity or lack of change, but rather a smoothly varying process.

4. Ibid., p. 23.
5. Ibid., p. 14.
6. August Strindberg, "Author's Foreword" to *Miss Julie*, in *Six Plays of Strindberg*, trans. Elizabeth Sprigge (Garden City, N.Y.: Doubleday, 1955), p. 63.
7. Antonin Artaud, *The Theatre and Its Double*, trans. Mary Caroline Richards (New York: Grove, 1958), p. 77.
8. Holtan, *Mythic Patterns*, pp. 33-34.
9. T. S. Eliot, "Christopher Marlowe," in *Essays in Elizabethan Drama* (New York: Harcourt, Brace, 1956), pp. 57-58.
10. W. B. Yeats, from *Autobiographies*, in *Henrik Ibsen: A Critical Anthology*, ed. James McFarlane (Baltimore, Md.: Penguin, 1970), p. 197.

Chapter 3: *Brand* and *Peer Gynt:* Ibsen's *Either/Or*

1. Northam, *Ibsen: A Critical Study*, pp. 5-6.
2. For years *Peer Gynt* was known to the rest of the world only through Grieg's orchestral suite. Originally writing it as incidental music for an actual production, Grieg later rewrote it for orchestra because he felt that the play would never become popular outside Norway, since it was essentially a satire directed at Norwegians. Actually, as I shall attempt to show, he was overestimating the Aristophanic nature of the play; Ibsen's aim went beyond the parochial. But Ibsen's long-lasting reputation as a social critic made it difficult for anyone to see *Peer Gynt* as anything but very specific satire.
3. Eric Bentley has noted that "Ibsen likes doctors." A doctor appears in almost every one of Ibsen's plays, and is usually characterized as basically good. Ibsen himself worked for a pharmacist in his youth, and considered entering medical school.
4. Letter to Magdalene Thoresen, 3 December 1865. Quoted in Michael Meyer, *Ibsen: A Biography* (Garden City, N.Y.: Doubleday, 1971), p. 215.
5. *Letters of Henrik Ibsen*, p. 199.
6. Søren Kierkegaard, *Either/Or*, trans. David F. Swensen and Lillian Marvin Swensen (Garden City, N.Y.: Doubleday, 1959), 1: 20.
7. Ibid., p. 25.
8. Ibid., pp. 30-31.
9. Kierkegaard, *Either/Or*, 2: 259.
10. James Kerans, "Kindermord and Will in *Little Eyolf*," in *Modern Drama: Essays in Criticism*, ed. Travis Bogard and William I. Oliver (New York: Oxford University Press, 1965), pp. 192-208.
11. Søren Kierkegaard, *Concluding Unscientific Postscript*, trans. David F. Swensen and Walter Lowrie (Princeton, N. J.: Princeton University Press, 1941), p. 231.
12. Halvdan Koht, *Life of Ibsen*, trans. and ed. Einar Haugen and A. E. Santaniello (New York: Benjamin Blom, 1971), p. 60.

13. Chekhov had a publisher named Marx!
14. Koht, *Life*, pp. 204-5.
15. The first volume of Kierkegaard's *Either/Or* deals with the aesthetic man, and the second with the ethical, an order that is of course reversed with the two Ibsen plays.
16. Kierkegaard, *Either/Or*, 2: 169.
17. Bernard Shaw, *Selected Non-Dramatic Writings of Bernard Shaw*, ed. Dan H. Laurence (Boston: Houghton Mifflin, 1965), p. 232.
18. Henrik Ibsen, *Emperor and Galilean*, in *The Oxford Ibsen*, trans. and ed. James Walter McFarlane and Graham Orton (London: Oxford University Press, 1963), 4: 259.
19. Lyons, *Henrik Ibsen*, p. 76.

Chapter 4: The Ethical Leap: *A Doll House*

1. Meyer, *Ibsen: A Biography*, p. 662.
2. There have also recently been *two* films made from the play. Although generations of professors have taught *A Doll House* as *the* feminist play, extensive rewriting was necessary in both films to establish the Woman's Liberation theme.
3. Meyer, *Ibsen: A Biography*, pp. 443-45.
4. Kierkegaard, *Either/Or*, 2: 10.
5. G. Wilson Knight, *The Wheel of Fire* (Cleveland and New York: World, 1957), p. 3.
6. Eugène Scribe, *A Glass of Water*, trans. Dewitt Bodeen, in *Camille and Other Plays*, ed. Stephen S. Stanton (New York: Hill & Wang, 1964), p. 46.
7. Rolf Fjelde points out in the foreword to one of his editions of Ibsen's plays that Ibsen's stage directions are always given from the point of view of the *audience,* rather than from that of the actors. (*Ibsen: Four Major Plays* [New York: New American Library, 1965], p. xxxv.)
8. Michael Chekhov, *To the Actor: on the Technique of Acting* (New York: Harper and Row, 1953), p. 84.
9. Francis Fergusson, *The Idea of a Theatre* (Garden City, N. Y.: Doubleday, 1949), p. 160.

Chapter 5: The Aesthetic Life: *Ghosts*

1. Meyer, *Ibsen: A Biography*, pp. 466 ff.
2. Meyer suggests that "a woman can have syphilis without realizing it or suffering any particular discomfort. In other words, and this is a far more frightening explanation of Oswald's illness than the usual one, Mrs. Alving could have caught syphilis from her husband and passed it on to her son." (ibid., p. 488). This would be an intriguing solution, but unfortunately Meyer is confusing syphilis with gonorrhea. The signs of syphilis—a chancre

sore on the genitals, followed by a more general rash—are quite noticeable in both sexes.
3. Eric Bentley, "Ibsen, Pro and Con," in *In Search of Theatre* (New York: Vintage, 1953), p. 346.
4. Northam, *Ibsen: A Critical Study,* p. 78.
5. Ibid., p. 76.
6. This is more striking in performance than it might seem in print. Regina seems literally radiant as she enters the gloomy room carrying the lighted lamp, its glow illuminating her arms and face.

Chapter 6: The Validity of the Ironic Life: *An Enemy of the People*

1. As this is being written, Steve McQueen has just announced that he will star in a filmed version of the play. The director insists that they will "stick closely to the original"—the original in this case being the Arthur Miller adaptation!
2. Northam, *Ibsen's Dramatic Method,* p. 85.
3. John Gassner, *Masters of the Drama,* 3d ed. (New York: Random House, 1954), pp. 372-73.
4. Bentley, *In Search of Theatre,* p. 347.
5. Alan Reynolds Thompson, "Ibsen as Psychoanatomist," *Educational Theatre Journal* 3 (1951): 39.
6. *The Oxford Ibsen,* 4: 34-35.
7. Professor Fjelde has suggested, in corresponding with me, that Dr. Stockmann's northern tour of duty might just as well show a strong public conscience as early failure. There is no mention in the play of Dr. Stockmann's original reasons for going north, but there is no doubt that at the time of the play, after his return, he views his practice there as a fiasco. All his references to the north are derogatory, as when he describes the place as unworthy of his talents: "It would have done those poor starved creatures more good if they'd gotten a veterinary instead of someone like me" (p. 353).
8. Other examples of double-roomed settings are in *Ghosts, The Wild Duck,* and *Hedda Gabler. A Doll House* could be included if we consider the hall a second room.
9. Kenneth Burke, *A Grammar of Motives* (Berkeley and Los Angeles: University of California Press, 1969), p. 3. Italics in the original.
10. Ibid., pp. 3-5. Italics in the original.
11. See above, p. 38.

Chapter 7: Reflections on Art and Politics

1. Leighton M. Ballew, "The U.C.T.A. Production Lists Project Survey—1973-74," *Educational Theatre Journal* 28, no. 1 (March 1976): 97.

Bibliography

Principal Works Consulted

Artaud, Antonin. *The Theatre and Its Double.* Translated by Mary Caroline Richards. New York: Grove Press, 1958.

Auerbach, Erich. *Mimesis: The Representation of Reality in Western Literature.* Translated by Willard R. Trask. Princeton, N. J.: Princeton University Press, 1953.

Ballew, Leighton M. "The U.C.T.A. Production Lists Project Survey—1973-74." *Educational Theatre Journal* 28, no. 1 (March 1976): 97-105.

Barthes, Roland. *Le Degré zéro de l'écriture.* Paris: Éditions du Seuil, 1972.

———. *Essais critiques.* Paris: Éditions du Seuil, 1964.

———. *Mythologies.* Paris: Éditions du Seuil, 1973.

———. *Le Plaisir du Texte.* Paris: Éditions du Seuil, 1973.

———. *S/Z.* Paris: Éditions du Seuil, 1970.

Bentley, Eric. *The Playwright as Thinker.* Cleveland and New York: World, 1955.

———. *In Search of Theatre.* New York: Vintage, 1953.

Bradbrook, M. C. *Ibsen the Norwegian: A Revaluation.* London: Chatto & Windus, 1946.

Burke, Kenneth. *A Grammar of Motives.* Berkeley and Los Angeles: University of California Press, 1969.

Chekhov, Michael. *To the Actor: On the Technique of Acting.* New York: Harper and Row, 1953.

Clurman, Harold. *Ibsen.* New York: Macmillan, 1977.

Culler, Jonathan. *Structuralist Poetics: Structuralism, Linguistics and the Study of Literature.* London and Henley: Routledge & Kegan Paul, 1975.

De George, Richard and Fernande, eds. *The Structuralists from Marx to Lévi-Strauss.* Garden City, N. Y.: Doubleday, 1972.

Derrida, Jacques. *De la grammatologie.* Paris: Les Éditions de Minuit, 1967.

———. *L'Ecriture et la différence.* Paris: Editions du Seuil, 1967.

Downs, Brian. *Ibsen: The Intellectual Background.* Cambridge: Cambridge University Press, 1948.

———. *A Study of Six Plays by Ibsen.* New York: Octagon, 1972.

Egan, Michael, ed. *Ibsen: The Critical Heritage.* London: Routledge, 1972.

Ehrmann, Jacques, ed. *Structuralism.* Garden City, N. Y.: Doubleday, 1970.

Eliot, T S. *Essays in Elizabethan Drama.* New York: Harcourt, Brace, 1956.

Erlich, Victor. *Russian Formalism.* The Hague: Mouton, 1955.

Fergusson, Francis. *The Human Image in Dramatic Literature.* Garden City, N. Y.: Doubleday, 1957.

———. *The Idea of a Theatre.* Garden City, N. Y.: Doubleday, 1949.

———. Introduction to *Aristotle's Poetics,* trans. S. H. Butcher, pp. 1-44. New York: Hill & Wang, 1961.

Fjelde, Rolf. Foreword to *Ibsen: Four Major Plays,* pp. ix-xxxv. New York: New American Library, 1965.

———, ed. *Ibsen: A Collection of Critical Essays.* Englewood Cliffs, N.J.: Prentice-Hall, 1965.

Gassner, John. *Masters of the Drama.* 3d ed. New York: Random House, 1954.

Goethe, Johann Wolfgang von. *Faust, Parts I and II.* Translated by Bayard Taylor. New York: Washington Square Press, 1964.

Gray, Ronald. *Ibsen: A Dissenting View.* Cambridge: Cambridge University Press, 1977.

Gross, Roger. *Understanding Playscripts.* Bowling Green, Ohio: Bowling Green University Press, 1974.

Hawkes, Terence. *Structuralism and Semiotics.* London: Methuen, 1977.

Hegel, Georg Wilhelm Friedrich. *Hegel: Texts and Commentary.* Translated and edited by Walter Kaufmann. Garden City, N. Y.: Doubleday, 1966.

———. *Hegel, the Essential Writings.* Edited by Frederick G. Weiss. New York: Harper & Row, 1974.

———. *Hegel on Tragedy.* Edited by Anne and Henry Paolucci. Garden City, N. Y.: Doubleday, 1962.

Heiberg, Hans. *Ibsen: A Portrait of the Artist.* Translated by Joan Tate. London: George Allen and Unwin, 1969.

Holtan, Orley I. *Mythic Patterns in Ibsen's Last Plays.* Minneapolis: University of Minnesota Press, 1970.

Hornby, Richard. *Script into Performance: A Structuralist View of Play Production.* Austin, Texas and London: University of Texas Press, 1977.

Hurt, James. *Cataline's Dream: An Essay on Ibsen's Plays.* Urbana, Illinois: University of Illinois Press, 1972.

Ibsen, Henrik. *Brand.* Translated by Michael Meyer. Garden City, N. Y.: Doubleday, 1960.

———. *Ibsen: The Complete Major Prose Plays.* Translated by Rolf Fjelde. New York: Farrar, Straus & Giroux, 1978.

———. *Letters of Henrik Ibsen.* Translated by John Nilsen Laurvik and Mary Morison. New York: Duffield & Co., 1908.

———. *The Oxford Ibsen.* Translated and edited by James Walter McFarlane and Graham Orton. 8 vols. London: Oxford University Press, 1963.

———. *Peer Gynt.* Translated by Rolf Fjelde. New York: New American Library, 1964.

Jakobson, Roman. "Linguistics and Poetics." In *Style and Language,* ed. Thomas A. Sebeok, pp. 350-77. Cambridge, Mass.: M.I.T. Press, 1960.

———. *Selected Writings.* 4 vols. The Hague: Mouton, 1966.

Johnston, Brian. *The Ibsen Cycle.* Boston: G. K. Hall, 1975.

Kant, Immanuel. *Critique of Practical Reason and Other Writings in Moral Philosophy.* Translated by Lewis W. Beck. Chicago: University of Chicago Press, 1949.

Kerans, James. "Kindermord and Will in *Little Ejolf.*" In *Modern Drama: Essays in Criticism,* ed. Travis Bogard and William I. Oliver, pp. 192-208. New York: Oxford Universty Press, 1965.

Kierkegaard, Søren. *Concluding Unscientific Postscript.* Translated by David F. Swensen and Walter Lowrie. Princeton, N. J.: Princeton University Press, 1941.

———. *Either/Or.* Translated by David F. Swensen and Lillian Marvin Swensen. 2 vols. Garden City, N. Y.: Doubleday, 1959.

———. *Fear and Trembling* and *The Sickness unto Death.* Translated by Walter Lowrie. Combined in a single volume. Garden City, N. Y.: Doubleday, 1954.

———. *Stages on Life's Way.* Translated by Walter Lowrie. Princeton, N. J.: Princeton University Press, 1940.

Knight, G. Wilson. *Henrik Ibsen.* New York: Grove Press, 1962.

———. *The Wheel of Fire.* Cleveland and New York: World, 1957.

Köhler, Wolfgang. *Gestalt Psychology.* New York: Liveright, 1947.

Koht, Halvdan. *Life of Ibsen.* Translated and edited by Einar Haugen and A. E. Santaniello. New York: Benjamin Blom, 1971.

Langer, Susanne K. *Feeling and Form.* New York: Charles Scribner's Sons, 1953.

———. *Philosophy in a New Key.* New York: New American Library, 1962.

Lavrin, Janko. *Ibsen: An Approach.* London: Methuen, 1950.

Le Gallienne, Eva. "Ibsen, the Shy Giant." *Saturday Review* 54, no. 33 (August 14, 1971): 23-26.

Lyons, Charles R. *Henrik Ibsen: The Divided Consciousness.* Carbondale, Ill., and Edwardsville, Ill.: Southern Illinois University Press, 1972.

Macksey, Richard, and Donato, Eugenio, eds. *The Structuralist Controversy: The Languages of Criticism and the Sciences of Man.* Baltimore, Md., and London: The Johns Hopkins University Press, 1972.

McFarlane, James Walter, ed. *Discussions of Henrik Ibsen.* Boston: D. C. Heath, 1962.

———, ed. *Henrik Ibsen: A Critical Anthology.* Baltimore, Md.: Penguin, 1970.

Meyer, Hans George. *Henrik Ibsen.* Translated by Helen Sebba. New York: Ungar, 1972.

Meyer, Michael. *Ibsen: A Biography.* Garden City, N. Y.: Doubleday, 1971.

Mukařovský, Jan. *Structure, Sign, and Function.* Translated and edited by John Burbank and Peter Steiner. New Haven, Conn., and London: Yale University Press, 1978.

Northam, John. *Ibsen: A Critical Study.* Cambridge: Cambridge University Press, 1973.

———. *Ibsen's Dramatic Method.* London: Faber and Faber, 1953.

O'Casey, Sean. *Collected Plays.* 4 vols. London: Methuen, 1963.

Richards, I. A. *Principles of Literary Criticism.* New York: Harcourt, Brace & World, 1925.

Schechner, Richard. *Public Domain: Essays on the Theatre.* New York: Bobbs-Merrill, 1969.

Scholes, Robert. *Structuralism in Literature: An Introduction.* New Haven, Conn., and London: Yale University Press, 1974.

Schopenhauer, Arthur. *The World as Will and Idea.* Translated by R. B. Haldane and J. Kemp. London: Routledge & Paul, 1957.

Shaw, Bernard. *The Quintessence of Ibsenism.* In *Selected Non-Dramatic Writings of Bernard Shaw,* ed. Dan H. Laurence, pp. 205-306. Boston: Houghton Mifflin, 1965.

Stanton, Stephen S., ed. *Camille and Other Plays.* New York: Hill & Wang, 1964.

Strindberg, August. *Six Plays of Strindberg.* Translated by Elizabeth Sprigge. Garden City, N. Y.: Doubleday, 1955.

Synge, John Millington. *Playboy of the Western World.* Edited by Malcolm Kelsall. London: E. Benn, 1975.

Tennant, Peter. *Ibsen's Dramatic Technique.* Cambridge: Bowes and Bowes, 1948.

Thompson, Alan Reynolds. "Ibsen as Psychoanatomist." *Educational Theatre Journal* 3 (1951): 34-39.
Valency, Maurice. *The Flower and the Castle*. New York: Macmillan, 1963.
Weiss, Peter. *The Investigation*. English Version by Alexander Gross. London: Calder and Boyars, 1965.

Index

Aesthetic level, 66, 71–75, 76, 79–84, 96–98, 103–6, 108–9, 112, 115–18, 120–21, 123, 125–31, 133–38, 143, 145, 147, 152, 160–61, 163, 165–66, 168, 172–73, 175, 176
Ambiguity, 46–47
Animal imagery, in plays, 82–83, 88, 93, 103, 105, 106, 163, 165, 176–77
Archer, William, 17, 18, 19, 90
Aristotle, 13
Arnold, Matthew, 86
Artaud, Antonin, 45
Auerbach, Erich, 36–37, 38, 47, 56

Barrymore, Ethel, 121
Barthes, Roland, 19, 20
Beckett, Samuel, 20
Becque, Henri, 35
Bentley, Eric, 34, 120, 124, 149–50, 186 n
Bradbrook, M. C., 17, 90
Brand, 9, 26, 53–79, 81, 85, 86–88, 92, 94, 95–97, 98, 99, 102, 115, 120, 121, 145, 151, 152, 153, 159–60, 178
Brecht, Bertolt: alienation effect, 37, 181, 182; Epic Theatre, 34, 35, 44–45; money in drama, 175

Brieux, Eugène, 34, 44
Bullins, Ed, 50
Burke, Kenneth, 170–71

Chekhov, Anton, 35, 36, 50
Chekhov, Michael, 117–18
Comte, Auguste, 65
Continuity. *See* Realism
Coward, Noel, 183

Darwin, Charles, 65, 158, 176–78
Doll House, A, 9, 10, 13, 21–23, 26, 30, 34, 44, 46, 47, 51, 58, 87, 89–119, 120, 121, 122–23, 125, 134, 135, 140, 145–46, 147, 153, 160, 164, 178, 181, 183, 188 n
Downs, Brian, 17

Eliot, T. S., 27, 50
Ellis-Fermor, Una, 120
Emperor and Galilean, The, 85–86, 87, 163
Enemy of the People, An, 9, 13, 22, 26, 28, 30, 34, 44, 46, 47, 58, 85, 87, 89, 139, 147–79, 183
Ethical level, 66–68, 70–75, 79–82, 84, 96–100, 102–7, 112, 115–19, 123,

125, 129–34, 142–44, 145, 147, 160–61, 164, 167, 172–73, 175

Fergusson, Francis, 119, 120
Fjelde, Rolf, 9, 10, 42, 187 n, 188 n

Ghosts, 9, 10, 13, 26, 30–31, 34, 39, 41–44, 46, 47, 49–50, 86, 87, 120–46, 147, 153, 161, 188 n
Goethe, Johann Wolfgang von, 77, 92
Grieg, Edvard, 186 n

Hauptmann, Gerhart, 35, 50
Hedda Gabler, 34, 86, 183, 188 n
Hegel, Georg Wilhelm Friedrich, 25–27, 65–66, 69
Holtan, Orley, 18, 48
Humorous level, 68–69, 71–72

Ibsen, Henrik: and Brecht, 44–45, 182; and Hegel, 26–27; and Italy, 60–61; and Kierkegaard, 24–28; and medicine, 35, 128, 140, 186 n; and myth, 48; and performance, 29–31, 111–19, 140–45, 170–73, 182–84; personal life, 27–28, 60–61, 75–76, 89, 116, 122; and realism, 33–36, 40–52, 53, 55; reputation, 13–14, 17, 32, 47–48, 51, 89–90, 121–22, 147–48, 180–84; and Romanticism, 33–34, 53–88; and science, 61, 62, 155; and Well-made Play, 110–11. *See also individual play titles*
Ironic level, 68–69, 72, 75, 82, 97, 115, 118, 125, 130–31, 133, 137–40, 142–43, 145, 147, 160–69, 172–75

Jakobson, Roman, 14–16, 181
Johnston, Brian, 25–27, 30, 69
Jonson, Ben, 50
Joyce, James, 51

Kant, Immanuel, 67, 133
Kerans, James, 70
Kierkegaard, Søren, 24–28, 31, 59, 64–88, 93, 97, 102, 115, 119, 122, 125, 132, 133, 134, 143, 147, 160–61, 166, 168, 170, 171, 178, 182. *See also* Aesthetic level; Ethical level; Humorous level; Ironic level; Religious level
Kindermord theme, 70, 93, 136–37
Knight, G. Wilson, 17, 33, 103–4, 120
Koht, Halvdan, 75

Landers, Ann, 69
League of Youth, The, 85, 153–55
Le Gallienne, Eva, 25
Lévi-Strauss, Claude, 14
Light-dark polarity, 61, 73–74, 76, 92, 114–18, 143–45, 188 n
Living Theatre, The, 35, 36
Lyons, Charles R., 18, 87

McFarlane, James Walter, 9
McQueen, Steve, 188 n
"Mansion" style of theater (medieval), 40
Marlowe, Christopher, 50
Marvell, Andrew, 129
Marx, Karl, 65
Master Builder, The, 34
Meyer, Michael, 9, 187 n
Miller, Arthur, 183, 188 n
Mukařovský, Jan, 28–29

Northam, John, 17, 18, 30, 33, 53–54, 119, 137, 141, 148, 170
North-south polarity, 61, 88, 92, 105, 118, 145, 175

O'Casey, Sean, 50, 51
O'Neill, Eugene, 25, 50

Peer Gynt, 9, 26, 41, 53–55, 73, 76–88, 92, 93–94, 95, 106, 121, 126–27, 129, 135, 145–46, 148, 152, 163–65, 168–69, 176
Pillars of Society, 33, 87, 91
Pinter, Harold, 50
Pretenders, The, 27
Problem Play, 121, 122, 123

Realism, 13, 28–29, 33–52, 53, 55, 87, 91–92 ff., 108–9, 145, 182

Religious level, 66–68, 70–75, 147
Repetition theme, 82, 84, 129
Richards, I. A., 154–55
Romanticism, 13, 28–29, 33–52, 53–88, 92, 120, 122, 128, 181
Rosmersholm, 34, 48

Sardou, Victorien, 111
Saxe-Meiningen, Duke of, 173
Schopenhauer, Arthur, 69–70
Scientific determinism, 44, 45–46
Scribe, Eugène, 109, 111
Shakespeare, William, 15–16, 30, 40, 70, 98, 103–4, 134, 181, 183
Shaw, George Bernard, 17, 18, 19, 85, 90, 91, 117
Simon, Neil, 183
Sophocles, 27
Spencer, Herbert, 177
Stanislavski, Konstantin, 144, 148–50
Stock responses, 154–55
Storey, David, 50
Strindberg, August, 33, 36, 38, 41, 45, 50, 55, 109, 178
Structuralism, 14–32
Synge, John Millington, 51–52
Sinclair, Upton, 35
Stendhal, 68

Taine, Hippolyte, 65
Theatre of Fact, 34
Thompson, Alan Reynolds, 152
Tremblay, Michel, 50

Unity of Time, 41–43

Weiss, Peter, 34, 38–39
Well-made Play, 91, 109–11
Wild Duck, The, 48–49, 50, 147, 153, 188 n
Wilder, Thornton, 183

Yeats, W. B., 51–52

Zola, Emile, 34, 35, 36, 44